Simon Veness

T0270421

111 Places
in Orlando
That You
Must Not Miss

Photographs by Kayla L. Smith

emons:

Bibliographical information of the Deutsche Nationalbibliothek
The Deutsche Nationalbibliothek lists this publication in
the Deutsche Nationalbibliografie; detailed bibliographical data
are available on the internet at http://dnb.d-nb.de.

© Emons Verlag GmbH
All rights reserved
Text by © 2024 Simon Veness and Susan Veness
© Photographs by Kayla L. Smith, except see page 238
© Cover icon: shutterstock/warat42
Layout: Eva Kraskes, based on a design
by Lübbeke | Naumann | Thoben
Maps: altancicek.design, www.altancicek.de
Basic cartographical information from Openstreetmap,
© OpenStreetMap-Mitwirkende, OdbL
Edited by: Karen E. Seiger
Printing and binding: Grafisches Centrum Cuno, Calbe
Printed in Germany 2024
ISBN 978-3-7408-1900-2
First edition

Guidebooks for Locals & Experienced Travelers
Join us in uncovering new places around the world at
www.111places.com

Foreword

Orlando is a peculiar place. Most visitors never actually see "Orlando," instead spending all their time in the theme parks and areas like International Drive. That was us, too, at first. We arrived from different directions, but for the same reason – to vacation at those theme parks. Susan first visited in 1971, from Michigan; Simon in 1993 from England. Our individual obsessions with the destination eventually led us to meet on a discussion forum about the parks, and to conversations about Simon's book, a *Brit Guide to Orlando*, the result of his first visit. Susan had been expanding her own Disney expertise, and proved an ideal US researcher for the *Brit Guide*.

When Simon immigrated to Orlando in 2004, our relationship went from professional to personal, while our view of the city changed radically, even as Susan took our writing to a new level with her *Hidden Magic of Walt Disney World* book series.

Living here is significantly different to being on vacation, and we were acutely aware there was so much visitors – and even many locals – were missing, hence the chance to write what are, in effect, 111 stories about the city, was hugely compelling. And surprising. Not only did we get to dig into the back-stories of all these unique places, but we also discovered recurring threads of history, entrepreneurship, and originality that gave us a new appreciation for this multifaceted destination.

Now, having put it all together, we hope readers pick up on those threads that – we believe – bind "111 Places" into a coherent narrative of diversity and inclusivity, not to mention a new-found maturity in The City Beautiful. How else do you explain a bevy of Michelin Guide-rated restaurants and a bona fide world-class performing arts center, among other non-theme-park developments? Yes, we've seen Orlando grow up before our eyes – and that's what we love most.

Simon & Susan

111 Places

1 The Beacham

Downtown's haunted hot spot

Revelers at downtown's biggest nightclub could be forgiven for think-ing there's an old-time vibe to the modern face of The Beacham, originally built in 1921. It would be surprising if its heritage didn't harbor a wayward spirit or two, and not the kind they serve at the bar. After all, this was where the hangings took place.

The site was originally the County Jail, complete with hanging post and graveyard. It served its purpose until ex-mayor Braxton Beacham (1864–1924) bought the lot, demolished the building, and constructed Orlando's first theater. Sadly, Mr. Beacham never thought to relocate the graveyard, leading to regular rumors of unhappy spirits appearing back-stage at odd moments – not ideal when acts included stars like W. C. Fields and The Ziegfeld Follies. Intrigue also surrounded the cross-street tunnel to the Angebilt Hotel. Stars reportedly accessed the theater through the tunnel to avoid being seen by the public, while others insisted it was a secret store for hooch during Prohibition. Yet another report claimed its underground corridor was connected to the mysterious death of a 1930s Vaudeville performer.

Over time, declining audiences led to disrepair and decay, and the building cycled through various uses, from concert venue for the Great Southern Music Hall to laser light shows and dinner theater. It was saved from the wrecking ball in 1987, and a nightclub opened in 1988, which quickly gained a mass following, hosting the "Summer of Love" in 1991–1992 with all-night dance parties and creative DJs.

After various disco incarnations, it became simply The Beacham in 2011. It has held the honor of downtown's top hot spot ever since, with a potent mix of live performers and popular DJs, including Tori Amos, Lauryn Hill, and Paul Oakenfold. Stories of ghostly appari-tions remain, though, including sightings of an old woman lurking by the side of the stage.

Address 46 N Orange Avenue, Orlando, FL 32801, +1 (407) 648-8363, www.beachamorlando.com | *Getting there* SunRail to Church Street; bus 3, 7, 11, 13, 15, 18 to N Orange Avenue & W Jefferson Street | *Hours* See website for events schedule | *Tip* Sample more nightclub buzz at The Vanguard, where the renovated historic Firestone Building offers a state-of-the-art light and sound system (578 N Orange Avenue, www.thevanguard.live).

2 — Beer Spa Orlando

Soak your cares away in a vat of suds

When bathing your liver in cold brewskis isn't quite enough to achieve a state of relaxation, it's time to pop into a wooden vat filled with warm beer-making ingredients, plus antioxidants, and give your whole body a good, long soak – with a chilled mug of local beer in hand.

Barbara Corzo and her husband Kevin Ortiz were traveling with friends in Europe. They were looking for something relaxing to do after two weeks of touring, and that something was a beer spa in Prague. It was so much fun that Corzo and Ortiz wondered why they couldn't get something similar in the US. They had not even left the spa when Barbara said, "We're doing this!" They invested, along with Corzo's sister and a friend of theirs, and secured an Orlando location. Barbara found an architect to give the spa an old-world feel with the benefit of modern touches and ADA compliance, and Orlando Beer Spa opened in summer 2021.

It's the only beer spa on the East Coast, and the only one in the country that is based on the traditional European style. But the real benefit of the 60-minute pampering is that each of the spa rooms is completely private, with two beery soaking tubs, an infrared sauna, and a full restroom. Even better, there's a dedicated self-serve beer tap for unlimited refills of IPA, pilsner, and Belgian witbier, or, for an additional fee, prosecco and cabernet sauvignon. And what better way to wind down at the end of spa time than luxuriating on a cooling bed made of soft, fragrant hay, because, yes, that's part of each package, too. For the optimum use of your time, spend 35 minutes in the tub, 10 minutes in the sauna, and then lay a sheet down and chill out on the hay bed. Tubs are emptied and cleaned after every use.

Two people can fit into each tub, and swimsuits are optional here. Sharing the experience with someone else makes for a unique, small-group bonding experience.

Address 11787 International Drive, Suite 106, Orlando, FL 32821, +1 (407) 778-1772, www.mybeerspa.com | Getting there Bus 8 to International & Riveroaks Bay Drives | Hours Wed–Mon 11:30am–7:30pm | Tip Can't get enough of the Beer Spa's brews? Visit the Tasting Room at Ivanhoe Park Brewing Company, the brewery that crafts them (1300 Alden Road, www.ivanhoeparkbrewing.com).

3 Black Hammock Bee Farms

Bee rescue with a sweet ending

Black Hammock Bee Farms in Oviedo, 18 miles northwest of downtown Orlando, became a glimmer in Dennis Langlois' eye in 2003 when a bee colony set up housekeeping in the yard of his and wife Beth's friend. Dennis rescued the swarm, and that extraction ended in a full-time career for the couple, whose goal was to save pollinators through bee-keeping education. Dennis fell in love with bees, became known as "The Bee Guy," and began extracting swarms for relocation.

When a great aunt left her property in the Black Hammock wilderness to the couple in 2005, Beth, with a baby on the way and a job as a florist, had no intention of moving there. Today, however, she's all-in, along with their son, helping anyone interested in apiculture to set up and maintain their own bee hives.

Each year, Black Hammock Bee Farms rescues more than 500 colonies that would otherwise be lost – from outdoor swarms to colonies inside the walls of houses – and gives them a new home in which to thrive. More importantly, the bees can continue their work as pollinators during a time when pollinators are in decline. Rescued bees are "loaned" to local farmers, helping increase their crop output tenfold.

Education is a big part of the business, including adult classes and classes for homeschoolers and other groups. Kids get to taste various types of honey, such as orange blossom, palmetto, gallberry, wildflower, and Brazilian pepper. Then they can put on bee suits to see where Black Hammock gets its raw, unfiltered honey. Visit the farm and its rescue yard, take an educational tour (minimum of 15 guests) or a bee-keeping class, and check out the Honey House to stock up on the best honey you'll ever eat, knowing your purchase will be as eco-friendly as it is tasty.

Address 2385 Howard Avenue, Oviedo, FL 32765, +1 (407) 330-8542, www.blackhammockbeefarms.com | **Getting there** By car, take toll road FL-417 north to exit 44, turn right onto FL-434, left onto Hammock Lane, then left onto De Leon Street. Continue to Howard Avenue and turn right. Proceed for two miles, and the venue is on the right. | **Hours** Tue–Fri noon–5pm, Sat 10am–3pm | **Tip** Revel in nature's beauty at Black Hammock Wilderness Area, where you might spot gray foxes, deer, wild turkeys, or gators along the 4.5-mile round trip hiking trails (3276 Howard Avenue, Oviedo).

4 __ Blue Jacket Park

Honoring Orlando's role in World War II

Today's stylish suburbs of Audubon Park and Baldwin Park once played a vital role in winning World War II, when the area was home to the Orlando Army Air Base and its supporting infrastructure. Starting in 1940, the base cranked out the military men and women and fighter pilots who would help bring down Adolf Hitler and his Nazi Germany war machine. It closed down in the mid-1960s and would be replaced with the Naval Training Base's Recruit Training Center in 1968.

The Training Center held the distinction of being the nation's first co-educational Navy boot camp, ultimately training and graduating more than 188,000 female recruits and 464,000 male recruits. Along with the Recruit Training Command Center, the 1,128-acre property included a Naval Hospital, Service School Command, and a Naval Nuclear Power Training Command.

The only reminders of Baldwin Park's wartime history are three sculptures. Navy veteran and sculptor Stanley Bleifeld's bronze *Lone Sailor* monument was dedicated in 2017 in the city's Blue Jacket Park, formerly the Naval training and graduation grounds and named for the sailors' sobriquet, "Blue Jackets." The *Blue Jacket Recruit*, the statue of a female bootcamp graduate and affectionately nicknamed "Sparky," was created by Navy veteran J. Don Reynolds and added to the park in 2018. And a 10-panel Navy History Wall memorial tells the sailors' stories through text and photo panels.

While casting the *Lone Sailor* statue, Bleifeld included relics from US Navy ships USS *Biloxi, Constellation, Constitution* (better known as "Old Ironsides"), *Hartford, Maine, Hancock, Ranger,* and nuclear submarine USS *Seawolf.* Reynolds added brass artifacts to the *Blue Jacket Recruit* from decommissioned American warships USS *Constellation, Independence, Lexington,* USS *Oriskany, Ranger, Saratoga,* and *Yorktown,* also known as the "Fighting Lady."

Address 2501 General Rees Avenue, Orlando, FL 32814, +1 (407) 246-2283, www.orlando.gov/Parks-the-Environment/Directory/Blue-Jacket-Park | Getting there Bus 6, 13 to General Rees Avenue & Glenridge Way | Hours Daily 6am–11pm | Tip A plaque honors the B-52 bomber crew who crashed after departing Orlando International Airport during its service as McCoy Air Force Base (Intersection of Conroy Road and Merriweather Drive).

5 Bob Ross' Grave

A happy final resting place

Would-be painters and college kids who weren't tuned in to *SpongeBob SquarePants* during their non-class hours watched with fascination bordering on mild cultism as artist Bob Ross (1942–1995) created landscape-inspired oil paintings filled with "happy little accidents" during his half-hour television show, *The Joy of Painting*. Although the program only ran from 1983 until 1994, Ross' celebrity really took off in re-run form, thanks to his gentle voice, massive mushroom-shaped, permanent-waved afro and matching facial hair, and his delightful penchant for spouting wise and amusing quips while he worked.

Born in Daytona and raised in Orlando, Robert Norman Ross encouraged would-be painters who tuned in to the show to view every mistake in their work as an opportunity. His own pieces transformed into complex nature-scapes as he stroked, stippled, and blended his way through each composition, usually incorporating the gentle curvatures of a snow-capped mountain range, a rustic cabin, a tranquil river or lake, and, of course, "happy little trees." As visually pleasing *objets d'art* came to life beneath his brushes, Ross' reassuring tone provided a calming backdrop. The combination made *The Joy of Painting* feel like 30 minutes of therapy with a mild sedative, only better.

Ross succumbed to lymphoma at the age of 52, but fans can still visit their artist idol at Woodlawn Memorial Park in Gotha. His fans often leave brushes, small paintings, and other tokens of affection on his elaborate grave marker (in the second row from the road, to the left of the Section O sign, nine headstones over). If paying your respects isn't enough, take a road trip to 757 E Third Avenue in New Smyrna Beach, Florida, where the Bob Ross Art Workshop & Gallery teaches the artist's *alla prima* – better known as "wet on wet" – style of painting in a room adorned with Ross' original artworks.

Address 400 Woodlawn Cemetery Road, Gotha, FL 34734, +1 (407) 293-1361 | Getting there By car, from Florida's Turnpike take exit 265 to East-West Expressway (SR-408). Take exit 2, then turn left onto Good Holmes Road, right onto Old Winter Garden Road, left onto Woodlawn Cemetery Road, and right into the cemetery's second entrance then proceed past the towered mausoleum. | Hours Daily dawn–dusk | Tip Bob's unique hairstyle earned him a public-art mural by artist Never in Winter Park. Find it on the side of Floyd's 99 Barbershop (610 West Fairbanks Avenue, www.floydsbarbershop.com/winter-park).

6 Bösendorfer Pianos
Musical masterpieces at the Grand Bohemian

The Grand Bohemian, Downtown Orlando's flagship hotel, is an icon in its own right, an elegant repository of art, hospitality, and fine cuisine. But the hotel's secret ingredient is a pair of musical instruments that often take visitors by surprise with their visual magnificence and captivating sound. They are two top-of-the-range Bösendorfer pianos from the private collection of hotelier and art aficionado Richard Kessler.

The Rolls-Royce of piano makers, Austria's Bösendorfer company dates back to 1828 and has been the manufacturer of choice for luminaries such as composer Franz Liszt, performers Victor Borge, Frank Zappa, and Tori Amos, and collectors like Grand Bohemian founder Kessler, who needed a centerpiece for his forthcoming Orlando hotel in 2001. Thanks to connections with the local Bösendorfer retailer, the hotelier acquired an ultra-rare model that immediately gave its name to the hotel's stylish cocktail lounge, serving as the crowning glory of a wealth of artwork that remains the Grand Bohemian's trademark.

The piano was also the cause of an impromptu concert in 2014, when a visiting musician discovered it purely by touch and asked the manager if he could play it. The musician was blind Italian tenor Andrea Bocelli and, of course, the manager said yes.

Kessler's original purchase has since been withdrawn, but the hotel still offers two models for piano fans to enjoy. The Bösendorfer Concert Grand sits in the Rotunda adjacent to the cocktail lounge. A rare Bösendorfer 290 Imperial on the fifth floor boasts 97 keys instead of the usual 88 as the design mark of Italian composer Ferruccio Busoni (1866 – 1924) in 1909. Just look for the all-black keys at the bass end (left) of the keyboard. Guests can enjoy the rich sound of the piano in the Rotunda every Friday and Saturday evening for the Bohemian Sonata, and also during Jazz Brunch each Sunday.

Address 325 S Orange Avenue, Orlando, FL 32801, +1 (407) 313-9000, www.kesslercollection.com/bohemian-orlando | Getting there By car, from I-4 E, take exit 83 for South Street. Cross South Street to S Garland Avenue, and then turn right on W Church Street. Turn right on S Orange Avenue, and the hotel is on the left. | Hours Daily 11am – midnight | Tip Need a Bösendorfer of your own? Atlantic Music in Melbourne is one of the country's leading piano dealers, and they will open an Orlando store in 2025 (150 East Drive, Melbourne, www.amcpiano.com).

7 __ Boxi Park

Lake Nona's social center

What do you do with 14 empty, discarded, full-size metal shipping containers? If you're imaginative, you stack them and refit them with kitchens, bars, and even a stage, and – hey presto – you have a viable, environmentally friendly, outdoor community venue. As a result, Lake Nona's Boxi Park has become the nightlife capital of southern Orlando, a laid-back party place in an area that previously had nothing to boast about.

As with most of the growth associated with high-tech Lake Nona, Boxi Park is the brainchild of international investors the Tavistock Group via their Restaurant Collection, which features an array of original dining and nightlife creations across the US. Orlando boasts four Tavistock venues, and Boxi Park is their crown jewel, an eye-catching combination of food-hall style with an outdoor feel that really comes alive on weekends. It was established in 2018 at the height of Lake Nona's main construction period – by far the biggest suburban development in the greater Orlando area – and quickly generated a vibrant dining and entertainment scene, featuring live music, cocktails, and chef-driven food concepts. It borrows from the food truck genre with its collection of counter-service outlets, such as Canonita Street Taqueria, Fowl Play, and the delicious burgers of The Grill Next Door. But it goes several steps further in creating a purpose-designed and cohesive setting for them and adding community-focused elements, like the sand volleyball court and dog park.

Visit on a Friday or Saturday evening for the best of the Boxi vibe, when the music stage is in full swing, and the food and drink outlets are all open. Don't miss the signature seafood sandwiches of Claw & Order, the sweet treats of Before It Melts, and margaritas of La Cajita. This venue is the ideal spot for special events, like St. Patrick's Day, Fourth of July, and New Year's Eve.

Address 6877 Tavistock Lakes Boulevard, Orlando, FL 32827, +1 (407) 536-9666, www.boxiparklakenona.com | **Getting there** Bus 418, 612 to Lake Nona & Tavistock Lakes Boulevards | **Hours** Thu & Fri 5–11pm, Sat noon–11pm, Sun noon–9pm | **Tip** For another creative Tavistock Collection venue, visit nearby Canvas Restaurant & Market, where the weekend brunch ambiance is superb (13615 Sachs Avenue, www.canvaslakenona.com).

8 _Bunk Baxter_ Statue

The cowboy who wrestled alligators

Saturday visitors to Orange Avenue in downtown Orlando in the mid-1880s would have been greeted by the sight of scruffy rancher Francis "Bunk" Baxter wrestling with an alligator. The entrepreneurial cowboy took advantage of "Cracker Day" each week to parade his gator-grappling bravado for out-of-town folks who came to do their shopping. Like many ranchers of that era, Baxter caught and skinned gators to protect his cattle. But he was savvy enough to know that if he demonstrated his wrangling skills for all to see, it was the equivalent of taking out a billboard ad for his ranch and meat market, as everyone wanted to know who this local daredevil was.

The rancher was subsequently immortalized in an 1880s photo of Orange Avenue that artist Scott R. Shaffer used in 1999 to create his life-sized, bronze sculpture of the man himself wrestling an alligator that now stands in front of the Orange County Regional History Center.

The larger-than-life Baxter may have passed into legend, but alligator wrangling remains a skill that Central Florida ranchers still need occasionally to prevent cattle from becoming gator fodder around lakes and watering holes. It is a talent visitors can see demonstrated on a daily basis by the wranglers at Gatorland and serves to underline Florida's original cattle-ranching pedigree, dating back to the state's European settlement in the 16th century.

The Floridian ranching style is also the primary origin of the word "cracker." The state's cowboys used whips to drive their cattle, and the crack of their whips led people to call them crackers. Cattle-ranching was the state's primary economic activity in the 19th century, and the likes of Baxter played a fundamental role in the development of places such as Orlando and Kissimmee. Modern-day cowboys who follow in their footsteps also claim the term "cracker" as a badge of honor, not mockery.

Address Heritage Square Park, 65 E Central Boulevard, Orlando, FL 32801 | **Getting there** Bus 60 to N Magnolia Avenue & E Central Boulevard | **Hours** Unrestricted | **Tip** The Osceola County Welcome Center & History Museum showcases more about the Baxter era cattle industry in Central Florida (4155 W Vine Street, Kissimmee, www.osceolahistory.org/ochs-welcome-center).

9   Casa Feliz
The house that sparked an uprising

To incite a citizens' revolt in tony Winter Park takes some doing. It's about as likely as the AARP staging an all-night rave. But that was the scenario in 2000, when the owner of a historic home planned to demolish it and build anew. "Oh no," said the locals. "You can't do that to our beloved Casa Feliz. That's a community treasure."

True, the home had been a social hub practically since it was built in 1933. It was a rare gem of design from renowned architect James Gamble Rogers II, a 100-year-old Spanish farmhouse concept that featured repurposed brick walls from the old Orlando Armory, wooden beams, and rustic tiled roof. It was also the crown jewel of the "City of Homes," earning the name "Casa Feliz," or "Happy House," in the 1960s, when it was often the center of Winter Park gatherings. Demolition had already begun when a hastily-created conservation society managed to get a temporary preservation order, thanks to a protected bald eagle's nest nearby. As protests against the house's destruction grew, the owner finally agreed to sell the structure – but not the land on which it stood.

"OK," said the locals. "We'll move it." And move it they did, all 750 tons of it, fully 300 yards from its original Lake Osceola site to municipal land on the Winter Park Golf Course. The entire house was painstakingly raised on pilings and then winched along at 10 feet per hour to its new location, becoming a media sensation along the way, as camera crews eagerly gathered to observe this feat of engineering.

Today, Casa Feliz is Winter Park's "parlor," a gathering place for the city's glitterati for holidays, cultural events, weddings, and more. It is also a museum to its period creation, offering open houses twice a week and docent-led tours of its restored interior and gardens that continue to highlight the work of Rogers – and the happy community vibes he created.

Address 656 N Park Avenue, Winter Park, FL 32789, +1 (407) 628-8200, www.casafeliz.us |
Getting there SunRail to Winter Park; by car, from I-4 E, take exit 87. Go east on
W Fairbanks Avenue and turn left on Park Avenue and continue for half a mile. Casa Feliz
is on the right. | Hours Tue & Thu 10am–noon | Tip The dramatic Colonial Revival style
of First United Methodist Church of Oviedo was another Rogers II design, dedicated in
April 1957 (263 King Street, Oviedo, www.fcoviedo.com).

10 Cassadaga
The psychic capital of the world

In 1860, 12-year-old George Colby was baptized in the icy waters of his Minnesota hometown's frozen lake, rocketing his psychic abilities sky-high, much to the anger of his staunch Baptist parents. But it wouldn't be a surprise when his long-dead uncle revealed a prophecy to him: Colby's destiny was to found a spiritual community "in the South."

In 1875, prompted by his Native American spirit guide Seneca during a séance, Colby teamed up with fellow medium T. D. Giddings and, again at Seneca's urging, the two traveled south to Jacksonville, Florida. They caught the train to Blue Springs Landing, and Colby set off into the wilds of West Volusia County. There, in an area of pine forest, he discovered a site notable for its seven "uncommon hills," just as Seneca had described, and in 1894, he created the Southern Cassadaga Spiritualist Camp, 30 miles north of Orlando.

Today's spiritualist community has been dubbed "The Psychic Capital of the World," and consists of 55 homes, a church, seven parks, meditation gardens, a welcome center/bookstore, and, according to residents, several small "spiritual vortexes." It does not, however, have a cemetery. It does have a few urban myths, though, including one surrounding a brick funerary bench dubbed the "Devil's Chair." Those willing to summon Lucifer are said to hear an evil voice while sitting in the chair, and legend also has it he'll drink cans of beer left for him, without opening the top.

Cassadaga, which is on the National Register of Historic Places, bills itself as the oldest continually active religious community in the Southeast, and the spirit-curious are invited to visit and "discover the peace within." Mediums, healers, and teachers of spiritualist beliefs all take appointments, and there are church services in the Colby Memorial Temple each Wednesday and Sunday for all comers, regardless of religion.

Address 1112 Stevens Street, Cassadaga, FL 32706, +1 (386) 228-2880, www.cassadaga.org | Getting there By car, from I-4 E: Take exit 114, then turn left on Howland Boulevard, right on Dr. Martin Luther King Beltway, then right on Cassadaga Road, and continue for 1.7 miles. | Hours Mon–Sat 10am–6pm, Sun 11:30am–5pm | Tip Stop at the 1920s period Cassadaga Hotel, which is not affiliated with the camp but claims to be haunted by a cigar-smoking spirit named Arthur (355 Cassadaga Road, Cassadaga, www.hotelcassadaga.com).

11 Cathedral Church of St. Luke

The legacy of Thomas Jefferson's grandson

The imposing edifice of downtown's Cathedral Church of St. Luke is hard to miss, a towering Gothic-revival structure complete with spired bell tower, flying buttresses, stone portals, and arches. It is the epitome of a principal church, a classic house of worship for the Anglican Communion of Central Florida. But, for all its impressive status, the cathedral has had a challenging route to its current form from its historic 19th-century founding by the grandson of Thomas Jefferson.

In 1869, Orlando was barely an outpost in the 24-year-old state, with fewer than 1,000 hardy souls, but it was here that Francis Wayles Eppes arrived, fresh from founding Florida State University in Tallahassee. Eppes, the son of Jefferson's daughter Maria and a devout Episcopalian, set about organizing a formal congregation and holding services in his home. From those humble beginnings, St. Luke's Mission was formalized in 1881, and, although Eppes died that year, the church he paved the way for achieved parish status in 1884 and was the obvious choice for a cathedral in 1902.

A wooden church holding barely 200 was hardly suitable cathedral material, though, so plans were put in place in 1925 for a grand structure, only for the funds to be hit by the collapse of the 1920s land boom and the Great Depression. There was still enough to build the impressive nave, but the full design would take another 62 years to complete. It was finally dedicated in 1987 after two years of building, including enlarged sacristies and renewed sanctuary and nave. The carved oak pulpit is a memorial to the Reverend William Crane Gray, the first Bishop in 1893, while, fittingly, the stained-glass window in the narthex depicting St. Luke honors Eppes and his contribution to the church.

Address 130 N Magnolia Avenue, Orlando, FL 32801, +1 (407) 849-0680, www.ccslorlando.org | **Getting there** Bus 60 to N Magnolia Avenue & E Washington Street | **Hours** Services Wed 12:05pm, Sun 8am, 10:15am, 6pm | **Tip** The 1952-built St. James Catholic Cathedral is just one block away and features impressive Romanesque Revival architecture (215 N Orange Avenue, www.stjamesorlando.org).

12 Celebration

Disney's town of yesteryear

Walt Disney's original blueprint for his vast Orlando resort included an urban core where people lived and worked. But his bold vision largely died with him in 1966, and Walt Disney World developed along more traditional theme park lines. That is, until the late 1980s, when the company expanded its horizons and revived the community concept.

The town of Celebration was announced in 1991, and construction began three years later on company land close to the parks, with Disney's creative guidance and input from renowned engineering and design firms. The master plan was driven by the New Urbanism movement, promoting modern design based on traditional, nuclear town values, with shops, schools, parks, and services within walking distance. With shades of Norman Rockwell, homes would have front porches, white picket fences, and garages at the rear. Even manhole covers had to conform to the idealistic pattern.

Inevitably, there was controversy. Environmentalists railed at the destruction of marshlands, which Disney countered by creating its Wilderness Preserve. Disney then sold its stake in the town to a private company in 2004, creating further angst for residents anxious about home maintenance. But, amid the disputes, a genuine town emerged that had instant visitor appeal, with its beautiful lakeside setting, classic Main Street, graceful walking paths, golf course, elegant hotel, boutique shops, and desirable dining, including a location of the historic Tampa-based Columbia restaurant.

As a real living, breathing community there is no overt Disneyness about it, but it attracts its fair share of admirers, notably for special events like Independence Day and Halloween. The Holidays are a real specialty, with homes dressed in astounding lighting displays that draw thousands of visitors, ensuring Walt's original vision still holds a kernel of authenticity.

TRAVIS SWANN TAYLOR

111
PLACES IN
ATLANTA
THAT YOU
MUST NOT
MISS

KELSEY ROSLIN / NIC YEAGER

111
PLACES IN
AUSTIN
THAT YOU
MUST NOT
MISS

Photographs by Nic Yeager

ALLISON ROBICELLI

111
PLACES IN
BALTIMORE
THAT YOU
MUST NOT
MISS

Photographs by John Dean

HEATHER KAPPLOW / KEN WINOKUR

111
PLACES IN
BOSTON
THAT YOU
MUST NOT
MISS

Photographs by Alyssa Wood

111

111 PLACES
THAT YOU MUST NOT MISS

BRIAN HAYDEN

111
PLACES IN
BUFFALO
THAT YOU
MUST NOT
MISS

Photographs by Jesse Pitzler

AMY BIZZARRI

111
PLACES IN
CHICAGO
★★★★
THAT YOU
MUST NOT
MISS

Photographs by Susie Inverso

PHILIP D. ARMOUR

111
PLACES IN
DENVER
THAT YOU
MUST NOT
MISS

Photographs by Todd Tumey

BRIAN JOSEPH

111
PLACES IN
HOLLYWOOD
THAT YOU
MUST NOT
MISS

DANA JOS TERROS / JONI FINCHAM

111
PLACES IN
HOUSTON
THAT YOU
MUST NOT
MISS

Photographs by Peter Jackson

LAUREL MOGLEN / JULIA POSEY

111
PLACES IN
LOS ANGELES
THAT YOU
MUST NOT
MISS

Photographs by Lucinda Evans

MICHELLE MADDEN
111
PLACES IN
MILWAUKEE
THAT YOU
MUST NOT
MISS
Photographs by Janet McMillan

FLORIANA PETERSEN
111
PLACES IN
NAPA &
SONOMA
THAT YOU
MUST NOT
MISS
Photographs by Steve Werney

JO-ANNE ELIKANN/SUSAN LUSK
111
PLACES IN
NEW YORK
THAT YOU
MUST NOT
MISS

CRISTYLE WOOD ELITTO
111
PLACES IN
PALM BEACH
THAT YOU
MUST NOT
MISS
Photographs by Jakob Takos

111
EXPLORE THE WORLD
RIGHT OUTSIDE YOUR DOOR!

BRANDON SCHULTZ
111
PLACES IN
PHILADELPHIA
THAT YOU
MUST NOT
MISS
Photographs by Lucy Baker

FLORIANA PETERSEN
111
PLACES IN
SAN FRANCISCO
THAT YOU
MUST NOT
MISS
Photographs by Steve Werney

HARRIET BASKAS
111
PLACES IN
SEATTLE
THAT YOU
MUST NOT
MISS
Photographs by Cortney Kelley

FLORIANA PETERSEN
111
PLACES
IN SILICON
VALLEY
THAT YOU
MUST NOT
MISS
Photographs by Steve Werney

ELIZABETH FOY LARSEN
111
PLACES
IN THE
TWIN CITIES
THAT YOU
MUST NOT
MISS

ANDREA SEIGER
111
PLACES IN
WASHINGTON
THAT YOU
MUST NOT
MISS
Photographs by John Dean

Address Market Street, Celebration, FL 34747, +1 (407) 566-4007, www.celebrationtowncenter.com | Getting there By car, from I-4 W: Take exit 64 for Highway 192 east. Take 192 to Celebration Avenue. Turn right on Celebration Avenue and continue to Water Street. Turn left and Water Street leads into Market Street. | Hours Unrestricted | Tip The 1996 Celebration Golf Club was the last course legendary designer Robert Trent Jones, Sr. worked on with his son before he died in 2000 (701 Golf Park Drive, Celebration, www.celebrationgolf.com).

13 Church Street Station

When downtown really rocked

In 1985, the four biggest attractions in Florida were Walt Disney World, SeaWorld, Busch Gardens, and Church Street Station. The theme parks have gone on to greater things, but not so Church Street Station. The multi-venue entertainment complex is only a shadow of its former self, despite drawing 1.7 million visitors annually in its hey-day. Much of the traditional bar and nightclub infrastructure remains, including the historic Cheyenne Saloon, but the essence of this live music dynamo is a fading memory.

Exactly how it went from boom to bust is a story couched in mismanagement and acrimony, including five years under the ownership of boy-band impresario – and serial con-man – Lou Pearlman. But it shined brightly during its time in the spotlight, from its 1972 debut until the mid-1990s, when competition from Disney and Universal's entertainment districts siphoned business away from downtown.

The creation of Pensacola entrepreneur Bob Snow from a collection of ramshackle railroad buildings dating to the 1880s, Church Street Station burst into life with Rosie O'Grady's Goodtime Emporium and quickly expanded to both sides of the street, with restored and replica period architecture. It eventually featured five rollicking showrooms offering jazz, blues, country, rock, and pop, as well as lively bars, restaurants, shops, and midway games. Crucially, the ever-creative Snow sold the business in 1989 to start a venture in Las Vegas, and it was already in serious decline when Pearlman bought it in 2003, before he went bankrupt, and it was auctioned off.

Happily, there are still a handful of operators keeping the traditional Church Street night-time vibe alive, including the drag shows of Hamburger Mary's, while visitors can still peer through the windows of the classic Cheyenne Saloon and see where a young Garth Brooks, among others, played some of his early gigs.

Address 127 W Church Street, Orlando, FL 32801 | Getting there SunRail to Church Street; bus 60 to S Orange Avenue & E Church Street | Hours Unrestricted | Tip The epicenter of downtown nightlife has moved just a couple of blocks, to the Wall Street Plaza between Orange Avenue and N Court Avenue (25 Wall Street Plaza, www.wallstplaza.net).

14 The Citrus Tower

Central Florida's ultimate high-rise

Florida's famous flatness rarely deviates from its underwhelming topography, in which molehills can genuinely seem like mountains. With barely a hillock in sight, even a few stories can seem vertigo-inducing; hence, the historic Citrus Tower in Clermont truly earns its iconic high-rise distinction.

Built from 1955–1956, it far exceeded original plans for a 60-foot observation post, and it just kept growing. Finally topping out at 226 feet, the Tower isn't the tallest structure in the area, but it does have a secret advantage that ensures it can claim the accolade of the region's greatest elevation. With the hills of Clermont reaching a dizzying 317 feet above sea level to Orlando's scant 100, the tip of the eye-catching Tower crests at 543 feet above sea level, higher even than the 30-story skyscrapers downtown.

And a truly commanding view it offers – for 35 miles in every direction. The original owners saw the orange-striped monument as a gigantic billboard for the thriving local citrus industry, and it attracted half a million visitors a year in its pre-Disney hey-day, using the slogan "Built by Vitamin C and Florida tourism." The entry fee was 93 cents to take the elevator to the observation platform for the breathtaking 360-degree vista, and local legend insisted you could see 17 million citrus trees from the top – until three crippling freezes in the 1980s wiped out many farmers and devastated the industry.

The Tower has had several owners since, struggling to remain relevant in Clermont's fast-growing urban landscape, but latest owners Ralph and Maureen Messer have grand plans to reinvigorate it, including a restaurant, deli, and the replanting of citrus trees. It still offers imposing views over Lake Apopka, Disney, and even the Kennedy Space Center on a clear day, and it continues to look "down" on neighboring Orlando from its lofty perch.

Address 141 N Highway 27, Clermont, FL 34711, +1 (352) 394-4061, www.citrustower.com | Getting there By car, take East-West Expressway (SR-408) west to the Florida Turnpike and go north to exit 272. Turn left on Highway 50 to Highway 27 and turn right. The Tower is a mile north on the right. | Hours Mon–Thu 7am–10pm, Fri & Sat 7am–11pm, Sun 11am–10pm | Tip If you like the look of nearby Lake Minneola from the Tower, it also boasts lovely Waterfront Park, with a sandy beach, children's play area, and splash park (100 3rd Street, www.clermont fl.gov).

15 __ Colonel Joe Kittinger Park

The Vietnam veteran's tribute to fellow vets

Driving on the East-West Expressway, you've probably passed Colonel Joe Kittinger Park many times. And now it's time to stop and have a look inside this small, green space that sits in one corner of Orlando Executive Airport. Few make the journey to discover why a 1970s vintage F-4 Phantom is the park's centerpiece. But local resident and former US Air Force pilot Joseph William Kittinger had good reason to know all about the plane. It was the one he flew during his USAF service from 1950 to 1978, and today it pays tribute to those who fought in the Vietnam War.

The legendary Colonel Kittinger was intimately acquainted with the Southeast Asia conflict, having suffered 11 months as a prisoner of war after being shot down over Vietnam in 1972 on his third tour of duty. The daring pilot had already more than earned his share of honors, including being inducted into the National Aviation Hall of Fame in Dayton, Ohio, after becoming the first person to see the curvature of the Earth with his 1960 world record sky-dive from 102,800 feet. But his commitment to the Vietnam veterans' cause was immense. After the park was designated in his name in 1992 and then closed from 2008–2011 as part of a highway expansion project, the colonel raised funds to have a Phantom moved from Texas to Orlando and installed as a permanent marker to all those who fought in that war. At the dedication ceremony in 2014, Kittinger said he hoped it would help Vietnam vets feel their service was appreciated.

The park features the F-4 he flew on several missions, while also affording fabulous close-up views of small planes and private jets taking off from the airport. The park memorial highlights the colonel's contributions to American aviation as a true pioneer. Sadly, he passed in 2022, but his life was honored by an Air Force parachutist and a fly-over in the "Missing Man" formation.

Address 305 S Crystal Lake Drive, Orlando, FL 32803, +1 (407) 246-2121, www.orlando.gov/Parks-the-Environment/Directory/Colonel-Joe-Kittinger-Park | Getting there Bus 51 to Anderson Street & Sunrise Rive; by car, take the East-West Expressway (SR-408) east to Exit 12A to E Anderson Street and continue to S Crystal Lake Drive. Turn left, and the park is on the right. | Hours Daily dawn–dusk | Tip Discover more Vietnam War memorials and history at The Original Bunker museum and grounds, dedicated to all of Central Florida's military veterans (3400 N Tanner Road, www.originalbunker.org).

16 Dickson Azalea Park

Orlando's surprising urban jungle

If ever there was a location that told the story of the city's 20th-century heritage, it is Dickson Azalea Park, part natural jungle, part urban oasis, on the edge of downtown. Originally a watering hole for cattle herders, the park blossomed after its five acres of land were gifted to the city in 1924 by real estate developer and later state senator Walter Rose, who decreed they should be for public use.

The first thing the city did was build a new bridge in the middle of the park, which spanned the aptly named Fern Creek. It replaced a wooden version that had been struggling with increasing traffic. The elegant Washington Street Bridge was the first of its kind in Central Florida, an arched, reinforced concrete design that cost a handsome $10,400 and ultimately earned celebrated status as one of only three bridges in the state on the National Register of Historic Places.

The unique park needed help to survive the Great Depression, as it became seriously overgrown and was returning to full jungle status. So, the volunteer Civitan Club initiated a beautification project for an extensive reworking of the plants and water features. The Civitans recruited various local organizations, backed by the national Works Progress Administration – one of President Roosevelt's New Deal programs – to put it back on its feet, just in time for World War II, when it served as home for the Red Cross Defense Unit.

Since 1938, the park has also been popular with the Girl Scouts of Citrus, who take advantage of this rare urban space in which to study nature. Fittingly, the modern-day Scouts helped to unveil the 2014 historical marker for this lush setting, which was renamed in 1933 for civic leader Colonel Henry Hill Dickson, who had been instrumental in planting azaleas throughout the city in the 1920s. Its tranquil setting continues to exhibit the classic red, pink, and white blooms each spring.

Address 100 Rosearden Drive, Orlando, FL 32803, +1 (407) 246-2283, www.orlando.gov/Parks-the-Environment/Directory/Dickson-Azalea-Park | Getting there Bus 51 to E Robinson Street & Celia Lane | Hours Daily dawn–dusk | Tip Azalea fans can enjoy even more of their favorite shrub at Kraft Azalea Garden in Winter Park (1365 Alabama Drive, www.cityofwinterpark.org).

17 _ The Dinky Line

Railroad history on the Orlando Urban Trail

Florida is famously flat, and that makes for easy walking, biking, and jogging, especially along the Orlando Urban Trail, designed for people of all fitness levels to enjoy. The full trail is 12 miles long. But a two-mile section runs along the former, narrow-gauge tracks of the Orlando and Winter Park Railway, nicknamed "Dinky Line," meandering past lakes, parks, and urban settings.

The Dinky Line ran from Orlando to Winter Park, and, from its 1887 inception, it was plagued with disasters. Construction was delayed due to slipshod contractors and an outbreak of yellow fever. Coach derailments within the first two days of operation weren't exactly encouraging. Added to that was trouble with cows crossing the track and lumbering trains emitting excessive noise and choking smoke within the residential area it ran through. Derailments continued, and students from Winter Park's Rollins College played pranks when the line was extended to include a stop near the campus. The Dinky Line tracks were eventually torn up and hauled away in 1969. Then, in 2010, the city acquired the land the railroad once traversed.

Start your walk at the entry point off N Magnolia Avenue and reward yourself with a drink at one of Ivanhoe Village's restaurants in the final leg of the round-trip journey. Or begin at Dorchester Road for a one-way amble toward Ivanhoe Village. To find each entry point, look for round, blue signs with a black half-circle that reads *Orlando Urban Trail*. They're located near the intersection of N Magnolia Avenue and N Orange Avenue, on the south side of the SunRail train tracks, and about one-third of the way down Dorchester Street, heading east.

As you make a leisurely circuit along the Urban Trail, think of the train dubbed "Little Wiggle" that once chugged along the Dinky Line. Its two engines bore the then-dismissive monikers, "Tea Pot" and "Coffee Pot."

Address N Magnolia Avenue, Orlando, FL 32804, www.orlando.gov/Parks-the-Environment/Directory/Orlando-Urban-Trail | **Getting there** Bus 102 to N Orange & N Magnolia Avenues | **Hours** Daily dawn–dusk | **Tip** Dinky Dock Park along the shore of Lake Virginia, at the end of Ollie Avenue, pays homage to the Dinky Line and its former train station (410 Ollie Avenue, Winter Park, www.cityofwinterpark.org).

18 Disney History at OPL

The "hidden" Disney collection

A little-known section on the fourth floor of the Orlando Public Library houses a massive assemblage of Disney history, from press clippings, photos, and periodicals to art, books, and memorabilia, much of it provided by the Walt Disney Company archivist. These artifacts chronicle Walt Disney World from before it broke ground to the present.

The better part of four library stacks are stocked with books about the Disney theme parks; Imagineers such as Marc Davis, Claude Coats, and Kevin Rafferty; Disney philosophy; animation; trivia; and hidden magic. There are even four large binders filled with planning permits and information for the town of Celebration, and seven binders hold Epcot's codes for building, plumbing, electrical, mechanical, gas, and fire prevention.

Among the treasures on display is a late-1960s promotional book detailing plans for Phase One of Walt Disney World – called the "New Disneyland" park – that include concept drawings for the never-built Asian Resort and the original design of Disney's Polynesian Resort that bear little resemblance to it today.

Thirteen filing cabinets filled with items delving into Disneyland Paris, Dreamers and Doers Awards, general files regarding entertainment, television, films, video, copies of *Eyes & Ears* newsletters for Disney Cast Members, and mundane laws and legislation are here, too, along with a motherload of facts and figures about the Walt Disney World theme parks and their history.

It is such a vast archive of information that the library had to create a binder titled *The Disney Collection Vertical File Holdings*, which visitors can use to pinpoint the location of documents or articles they'd like to view. None of the items can be checked out of the library, and a librarian must open each cabinet for you. But if you're a die-hard Disney fan, this is the treasure-trove you've been looking for.

Address 101 E Central Boulevard, Orlando, FL 32801, +1 (407) 835-7323, www.ocls.info |
Getting there Bus 60, 62 to N Magnolia Avenue & E Central Boulevard | Hours
Mon–Thu 10am–7pm, Fri & Sat 10am–6pm, Sun 1–6pm | Tip In 1970, Disney company
first showed off its grand plan for Walt Disney World at a preview center that is now the
Amateur Athletic Union (1910 Hotel Plaza Boulevard, Lake Buena Vista).

19 Disney Wilderness Preserve

Nature's Magic Kingdom boost

When the Walt Disney Company announced its intention in 1991 to create the purpose-built town of Celebration, it provoked an outcry from environmentalists and wildlife conservationists. The nearly 5,000 acres of land included valuable wetlands and was home to much birdlife. Hence, it became a major conservation concern, even though Disney planned to keep half the acreage in its natural state. The answer to everyone's fears was the fledgling concept of mitigation banking.

To allow the Celebration development to go ahead, Disney bought up 8,500 acres of derelict farmland 27 miles south of the Magic Kingdom and, in conjunction with The Nature Conservancy and several state agencies, created a nature preserve dedicated to wetland restoration. It was one of the earliest – and largest – mitigation projects in the country, and it soon became an environmental *cause célèbre*, with its eco-friendly visitor center and learning facility, which include geothermal heating and cooling. In 2014, Disney purchased an adjacent, 3,000-acre parcel to prevent it from becoming a housing development, and the preserve became a poster child for habitat restoration, recognized by the Audubon Society, among others, for its wildlife and landscape renewal.

For visitors, the preserve represents nine miles of well-marked and tranquil hikes adjacent to Lake Russell, through rejuvenated longleaf pine forest and native scrubland that includes habitats for the gopher tortoise, Sherman's fox squirrel, Southeastern big-eared bat, wood storks, and the elusive red-cockaded woodpecker, as well as an array of important flowering plants. All non-native and invasive plants are ruthlessly rooted out. Be aware that the trails have some low-lying areas and can be seriously muddy after summer rains.

Address 2700 Scrub Jay Trail, Kissimmee, FL 34759, +1 (407) 935-0002, www.nature.org |
Getting there By car, from I-4 W take exit 58 and turn left on Osceola Polk Line Road.
Turn left on Highway 17/92 to S Poinciana Boulevard and turn right. Continue for
eight miles then turn right on Pleasant Hill Road. Turn left into Scrub Jay Trail. | Hours
Mon – Sat 9am – 4:30pm | Tip For more local nature and the thrill of an airboat ride,
visit the nearby Boggy Creek Airboat Adventures (2001 E Southport Road, Kissimmee,
www.bcairboats.com).

20 Disston Sugar Mill
The sad relic of a pre-Disney visionary

You'd think the man who made the biggest private land purchase in history would be memorialized throughout Florida. That his name would be synonymous with the areas he developed. That the area known as Orlando would have lauded him over the years. But Hamilton Disston and his incredible dream for Central Florida were all but forgotten.

Back in 1881, Florida was going bankrupt, the legacy of investing in railroad companies that had failed in the aftermath of the Civil War. Enter a visionary with big ideas decades before Walt Disney. The Pennsylvania industrialist arrived with an offer to buy four million acres of land, drain the swamps, build canals, and open the state for business. It was, *The New York Times* reported, "the largest purchase of land ever made by a single person in the world." And it worked. It brought in industrialists, railroads, and tourists. And though his grand canals didn't quite pan out, he still drained vast stretches of swampland that became prime commercial land, including the cities of Kissimmee and St. Cloud.

Disston also master-planned a Gulf Coast city that became today's Gulfport and built a modern sugar mill on drained land in the area of St. Cloud. His legendary Florida status seemed guaranteed – until the financial panic of 1893 wiped out the family fortune and saw Disston retreat to Pennsylvania. He died of heart disease in 1896 at the age of 51. His family abandoned his Florida ventures, selling them off for a pittance. His grand dream of a dynamic industrial future was over.

The one surviving remnant of Disston's era is the crumbling relic of his sugar mill, an ambitious, brick-built plantation that was allowed to fall into ruins but can still be accessed today by intrepid visitors to the unmarked site in a residential area of the city. It's hardly a fitting tribute, but it is a window onto a fascinating period of history.

Address Adjacent to 3901 Blackberry Circle, St. Cloud, FL 34769 | Getting there By car, take the Florida Turnpike south to exit 244. Turn left on Highway 192 for two miles to Commerce Center Drive. Turn left and continue to Blackberry Creek Drive. Turn left on Blackberry Circle and left again at the T-junction. The Mill ruins are just beyond the small parking lot. | Hours Unrestricted | Tip Ironically, there is a historical marker for the mill 1.5 miles away at the western end of St. Cloud Lakefront Park (2701 E Lakeshore Boulevard).

21 Dr. Phillips House

A philanthropist for the ages

You can't go far in Orlando without coming across the name. It's a high school; it's a hospital; it's a performing arts center; it's a whole residential area, including a popular shopping plaza. Dr. Phillips is seemingly everywhere in the city, yet few know his pivotal role in Florida history. His house, at least, is on the National Register of Historic Places.

Philip Phillips was born in Memphis, Tennessee in 1874 to wealthy parents, and earned a medical degree at Columbia University. Choosing farming instead of medicine, he decided Florida was the place to be, and, after one false start, entered the citrus industry in 1897. Within 30 years, his company was the largest of its kind in the world, with more than 18 square miles of groves in Orange County alone. He was a benefactor and innovator, introducing new techniques, including the pasteurization of orange juice, and good working conditions for employees.

Then, in 1954, he did an astounding thing. He sold out to Minute Maid for more than $50 million – half a billion in modern terms – and, until his death in 1959, he devoted his life to good causes, creating a hospital for the Black community, bankrolling social services, and giving millions to charity. His stately, 1893 downtown home, which he bought in 1912 and lived in for 47 years, became known as Philanthropy Central, and the good doctor was a byword for benevolence.

Sadly, the Phillips family have all passed, but the three-story Dr. Phillips House remains a testament to their patronage and altruism and a shining example of community generosity. It is now a popular wedding venue, as well as the sole surviving model of Shingle architecture in the city. It still boasts grand Victorian rooms, fireplaces, and classical-featured garden, complete with a gazebo, while paying tribute to the man who left an indelible philanthropic stamp on the region.

Address 135 N Lucerne Circle E, Orlando, FL 32801, www.drphillipshouse.com | **Getting there** Bus 7, 11, 18 to Rosalind Avenue & Anderson Street | **Hours** Unrestricted from outside only | **Tip** Check out The Wellborn hotel next door, with buildings that date to 1883 and 1917, respectively, including one that was moved several miles to this site (211 N Lucerne Circle E, www.thewellbornorlando.com).

22 Dubsdread Golf Course

The gamble that paid off – literally

Being Central Florida's oldest public golf course is a fair claim to fame. But that distinction pales compared to Dubsdread's historic founding and long family ownership, which has included a major feud, being buzzed by B-17 bombers, and playing host to some of the game's greats.

The creation of 1920s real estate mogul Carl Dann, Dubsdread resulted from a dispute over the then-common practice of on-course wagering. Dann belonged to the Country Club of Orlando, where, legend has it, snooty members took a dim view of gambling. As it was one of Dann's main reasons for playing, gambling became a major bone of contention, so much so, he decided to establish his own club – with his own rules. He did just that, canvassing support in downtown Orlando for a new course that was – gasp! – outside the city limits, practically in the boonies by the standards of the day.

Shrewdly, Dann also developed a housing estate alongside the course, giving the roads golf-related names like Putter Street and Niblick Avenue. The club was a roaring success, especially with gamblers, both on the course and over cards afterwards in the clubhouse. Snooty it definitely wasn't. During World War II, it was home to officers of the Orlando Army Air Force base, and it wasn't uncommon for bomber pilots to buzz the course before driving out to it for social events. After the war, golfing legends Ben Hogan, Sam Snead, and Byron Nelson were regular visitors. Dubsdread's future was assured.

The Dann family sold it to the city in 1978 and it was given a major facelift in 2007. Its Tap Room restaurant became a star in its own right for its award-winning, casual-chic cuisine. And that club name? Dann pieced it together from the 1920s term for novice golfers, "dubs," and the reputed "dread" they would often feel when confronted with a challenging course, proving, without doubt, he had a wry sense of humor.

Address 549 W Par Street, Orlando, FL 32804, +1 (407) 246-2551, www.historicaldubsdread.com | Getting there Bus 125 to Edgewater Drive & W Par Street | Hours See website for tee times. The Tap Room Mon–Sat 11am–10pm, Sun 10am–9pm | Tip For another one-of-a-kind course, try Winter Park Golf Course. Founded in 1914, it's the second oldest in the area and a rare nine-hole walking course (761 Old England Avenue, www.cityofwinterpark.org).

23 East End Market
Orlando's culinary incubator

Food entrepreneurs have played a big role in Orlando's diversification and growth in recent years. Many got their start at East End Market, the 2013 brainchild of real estate developer John Rife III, who wanted to encourage a local, sustainable food system. Building from his original creation of the Winter Park Urban Farm in 2008, which aimed to educate people about growing food in urban areas, Rife founded the Winter Park Harvest Festival, celebrating a grassroots movement of local farmers, gardeners, and food-related entrepreneurs. He recognized that he had a gastronomic tiger by the tail, which spurred him to investigate new ways to bring his passion fully to life. He realized that he needed to create a center for collective culinary creativity.

Buying and converting the overgrown site of an abandoned church, Rife quickly recruited a succession of foodie disciples for his cooperative venture, and East End Market was born. Since its foundation, the venue has rapidly matured into both a captivating neighborhood market and a showcase for individual artisans and chefs. Many have gone on to create exciting new restaurants of their own, such as Farm & Haus, the "healthy comfort foods" concept in Winter Park.

While there is a periodic turnover of vendors, regular offerings include a delicious array of freshly baked breads, a coffee roastery, artisan cheeses, a juice bar, and Domu, a Michelin-honored ramen restaurant. Behind the scenes, a commissary kitchen provides the collaborative space for most of the cooking. It's also where Rife continues to encourage experimental food programs and innovation. The loft-style market, with its captivating community vibe, has also been instrumental in the re-emergence of the Audubon Park Garden District, one of the city's many Main Street districts that speak to the nature of Orlando's vibrant urban profile.

Address 3201 Corrine Drive, Orlando, FL 32803, +1 (321) 236-3316,
www.eastendmkt.com, info@eastendmkt.com | Getting there Bus 6 to Corrine & Chapel
Drives | Hours Mon–Thu 8am–7pm, Fri & Sat 8am–9pm, Sun 8am–6pm | Tip The
poster child for East End Market "graduation" is cookie sensation Gideon's Bakehouse,
which has gone on to be a huge hit at Disney Springs (1486 Buena Vista Drive,
www.gideonsbakehouse.com).

24 Eatonville

"The town that freedom built"

Eatonville is the nation's first self-governing, all-Black municipality. Incorporated in 1887, it became home to hundreds of formerly enslaved people and has retained its proud sense of identity. After the 1863 Emancipation Proclamation, the new residents settled near what is now Maitland, working as laborers for white residents. Black citizens faced relentless prejudice as they tried to purchase acreage on which to create a community of "colored people."

It wasn't until white landowner Josiah Eaton sold a tract of land to New Yorker Lewis Lawrence that the glimmer of progress was realized. Of the 22 acres he purchased, Lawrence donated 10 acres to aid the freedmen's cause, and those acres would mark the starting point for the lot acquisitions that would become Eatonville. Then the work of creating a thriving town – with its own churches, schools, restaurants, and stores – out of the harsh Floridian scrubland began.

Eatonville's most famous resident is novelist Zora Neale Hurston (1891–1960), author of *Their Eyes Were Watching God*. Today, the one-room Zora Neale Hurston National Museum of Fine Arts, or The Hurston, honors her legacy and works by artists of African descent.

The corner of People Street and Kennedy Boulevard was once the location of Zora Neale Hurston's family home, and the grocery store mentioned in her novel once sat directly across Kennedy Boulevard (formerly Old Apopka Road). Eatonville's first church was at the corner of Kennedy Boulevard and East Street on land donated by Lawrence, where St. Lawrence A.M.E. Church is now located. Look for a mural of Hurston on the corner of Elizabeth and Lemon Streets, her friend Matilda's home at 11 Taylor Street, and the former site of Hungerford School, Central Florida's first African American school, at the end of College Avenue. Tragically, developers paved over the old cemetery at Eaton Street and East Avenue.

Address 344 E Kennedy Boulevard, Eatonville, FL 32751, +1 (407) 647-3307, www.hurstonmuseum.org | Getting there Bus 1, 9 to E Kennedy Boulevard & College Avenue | Hours Mon–Fri 11am–2pm; historical sites unrestricted | Tip Taste authentic Eatonville with award-winning Soul Food Fantasy's braised oxtails or shrimp with Cajun grits, washed down with Kool Aid (521 E Kennedy Boulevard, Eatonville).

25 Edgewater Hotel Chef's Table

From bass fishing to fine dining

Hollywood legends Clark Gable and Humphrey Bogart never shared the same movie screen, but, unlikely as it seems, they did both appear at the Edgewater Hotel in Winter Garden. According to local legend, they were lured by nearby Lake Apopka, "the large-mouth bass capital of the world." Today, visitors are lured to the historic 1927 hotel by the burgeoning Main Street vibe and a delightful fine-dining experience, featuring an ever-changing three-course prix fixe menu with optional wine pairings.

The Chef's Table opened in 2008 and has quietly become one of Florida's finest. Like modern Orlando, its origins lie in Walt Disney World. Not only did the hotel host construction workers for the hush-hush project in the 1960s, but it also attracted two Disney culinary glitterati to create the signature restaurant after the hotel's 2003 restoration. Local residents Kevin and Laurie Tarter were, respectively, the chef at renowned Victoria & Albert's and a respected server at Disney's other high-end restaurant, the California Grill. Together, they created a new vision for distinctive dining in the intimate confines of the hotel's former Western Union office, serving typical delicacies such as foie gras, pan-seared duck breast and veal *au poivre*, using the finest seasonal ingredients.

The Chef's Table now enjoys a prestigious Zagat rating alongside Victoria & Albert's, and the couple have expanded their restaurant expertise to the wine-bar style of the Attic Door, right across the street from the hotel. The Edgewater itself, fully restored as a boutique B&B, continues to delight a modern audience with period charms. Look for the manually operated elevator, antique fixtures, barbershop, and old-fashioned ice cream store that go with its 44 individually furnished rooms.

Address 99 W Plant Street, Winter Garden, FL 34787, +1 (407) 230-4837,
www.chefstableattheedgewater.com | **Getting there** By car, take the East-West Expressway
(SR-408) west to the Florida Turnpike. Take the Turnpike one exit to Highway 429, and
the 429 one junction to Exit 24, Plant Street. Turn left on Plant Street and continue for
two miles to the Chef's Table, which is on the right. | **Hours** Mon 4–9pm, Tue–Thu
4–10pm, Fri 4–11pm, Sat 11am–11pm, Sun 11am–9pm | **Tip** Winter Garden boasts
one of the best farmers' markets in Central Florida, open every Saturday (104 S Lakeview
Avenue, www.cwgdn.com/322/Winter-Garden-Farmers-Market).

26__Enzian Theater
Art-house cinema with a kick

Back in the 1980s, Orlando's reputation pretty much started and ended with Walt Disney World. Arts and culture were an afterthought, lost in the theme park rush. Enter the Tiedtke family in 1985, local philanthropists with a mission to give local culture a kick up the arts – and the Enzian Theater was born. At a time when US art-house cinema was waning, the Tiedtkes took the opposite view and created their own image of a thriving, community-based and celluloid-infused ethos.

Groups initially mounted pickets and protests outside the picturesque setting in suburban Maitland – including for the Enzian's temerity in showing an X-rated movie one time. But the theater quickly became a champion of free thinking, plowing a solo furrow for independent films and creating an open house for debate and dialogue. Patrons could enjoy a rare dine-in option for an upscale movie-watching experience, but it was the theater's ability to show 35-millimeter film as well as the digital variety that cemented its place as the state's leader in art-house offerings.

From those early days of demonstrations, the boutique picturehouse is now the home of the prestigious annual Florida Film Festival, as well as down-home touches like its Peanut Butter Matinee Family Film Series (free for under-13s) and Freaky Friday presentations, "a nose-dive into the weird, wild, and wicked world of genre films," as suggested by one of the staff. Amazingly, this "little cinema that could" is also one of only 60 festival hosts worldwide that enjoys Oscar-qualifying accreditation.

Even better, its lovely situation, including moss-draped oaks, bubbling fountain, and gracious courtyard, has ensured its popularity with the date-night crowd, thanks to the addition of its tiki-style Eden Bar, which features cocktails and late-night menu, as well as an impressive mural by Oscar-nominated animator Bill Plympton.

Address 1300 S Orlando Avenue, Maitland, FL 32751, +1 (407) 629-1088,
www.enzian.org | Getting there Bus 1, 9, 102 to S Orlando Avenue & Magnolia
Road | Hours See website for showtimes; Eden Bar Mon & Tue 4–11pm, Wed & Thu
11am–11pm, Fri & Sat 11–1am, Sun 11am–11pm | Tip Just 1.5 miles south is the visually
stunning Winter Park Library & Amphitheater by renowned architect Sir David Adjaye,
partly funded by the Tiedtkes (1050 W Morse Boulevard, www.winterparklibrary.org).

27 Fleet Farming

Fresh produce from your front yard

During times of crisis, people have often turned to home gardening to feed their families and sustain their communities. Fleet Farming gets ahead of looming crises – the decline in pollinator populations, the effects of fossil fuel consumption, and issues from lawn fertilizer run-off – on a yard-by-yard basis, while also providing much-needed fresh produce to food banks and areas known as "food deserts," where nutritious meals are harder to come by. Even better? It's all done through community volunteerism.

The company currently has a system of more than a dozen "farmlettes" in Audubon Park, one of which can be seen at the East End Market (3201 Corrine Drive) and another at Audubon Park Covenant Church on the corner of Cardinal Road and Lark Place. A drive around Audubon Park – especially along Chelsea Street, Heron Drive, and Osprey Avenue – reveals further farmlettes planted in homeowners' front yards.

Inspired by the idea of having fresh produce straight from your own yard, while also helping those in need through sharecropping? Fleet Farming works with any homeowner interested in starting their own micro-farm, assisting with crop selection appropriate to each yard's unique characteristics, installing raised garden beds, and continued cooperation with the homeowner toward successful, ongoing gardening.

If you don't have a yard in which to do edible farming but still want to be part of the Earth-friendly solution, you can join one of Fleet Farming's community "Swarm Ride" events. Using bikes pulling small trailers carrying farming tools, the least-polluting transportation, "swarms" visit the Audubon Park farmlettes to do routine maintenance to harvest produce when it's ready. Ninety percent of crop yield goes into the community. No more sneaking out under cover of darkness to leave all those extra tomatoes on your neighbor's front porch!

Address 3219 Chelsea Street, Orlando, FL 32803, www.fleetfarming.org | Getting there By car, take I-4 E to exit 84A. Turn left onto E Colonial Drive, left onto N Bumby Avenue, right onto Chelsea Street, then right again to stay on Chelsea Street, which becomes Cardinal Road. Look for the farmlette at Audubon Park Covenant Church. | Hours Unrestricted; see website for Swarm Ride events | Tip While exploring Audubon Park, notice the area's connection to the Audubon Society. Many of the streets are named for birds (www.orlando.gov).

28 Florida Glass House
The hottest date night in town

Learn the delicate art of creating something beautiful from molten glass during the Florida Glass House's one-on-one glassblowing workshops, guided by owner Thomas Musolino, whose 20 years of experience ensure participants create a successful finished product – and have a good time doing it.

Musolino began glassblowing in 2004, advanced to doing it professionally in 2007, and opened his business that same year, having left his career as a chef because, he says, "the work was too hot." Out of the frying pan and into the fire, he admits glassblowing is just as sweltering as the professional kitchen, but he enjoys it more, and that passion translates to the workshops he offers.

These classes aren't intended to teach people how to become a glassblower, though. The aim is to teach anyone aged eight and up enough to walk away with a beautiful piece of art.

Once you make your reservation for the one-hour workshop, you and the other participants watch a demonstration that gives you the basics, then you choose from a menu of 10 items you can create. Glass flowers and glass round ornaments are the most popular entry-level projects, flowers being more hands-on, while ornaments have the advantage of being able to be hung from a tree or a window. Then it's one-on-one after that, from gathering the glass, applying the color, getting up to the preliminary shape, and then doing the final shape. Along the way, Musolino performs the function of "training wheels on a bike." If the glass-blower's piece is leaning to one side or the other, he helps bring it back to the middle. If it's gone wonky, he helps keep it from falling over. He does the hard stuff so participants can do the fun stuff.

Bond over a shared experience with a Date Night/Bring a Friend package, or meet like-minded enthusiasts during the studio's weekly workshops. And remember, even Chihuly had to start somewhere.

Address 809 Virginia Drive, Orlando, FL 32803, +1 (407) 896-9116, www.flglasshouse.com | Getting there Bus 125 to Mill Avenue & Virginia Drive | Hours See website for class schedule; shop Tue–Sat 11am–4pm | Tip Be one of the cool kids and take an Instagram-worthy selfie in front of *The Glass House* by stained-glass artist Tom Fruin (13615 Sachs Avenue, Lake Nona, www.lakenona.com/thing-place/the-glass-house).

29 Fort Christmas
Orlando's Seminole frontier

In 1837, the US was entrenched in the second of its three Seminole Wars, a sorry sequence that was sparked by President Andrew Jackson's bid to have all Indigenous tribes forcibly moved west of the Mississippi.

Like many of Jackson's genocidal policies, it wasn't going well, as the Seminoles were a shrewd and elusive enemy. In late 1837 and tiring of the war, Jackson directed the Army to bring its full might to bear on the Native Americans. A 2,000-soldier column led by Brigadier General Abraham Eustis (1786–1843) arrived at a site 26 miles east of Orlando to create one of 200 forts as part of a statewide offensive. The war still dragged doggedly on, and it took another five years before the government decided to reach a negotiated settlement, allowing the Seminole survivors to stay in an informal reservation in South Florida.

A community quickly developed around the fort that Eustis left behind, and the unincorporated village of Christmas came into being. At the same time, the fortification itself was abandoned in 1838 and collapsed by 1845. More than 100 years later, in a bid to revive the period's history, the Fort Christmas Historical Society and Orange County Parks and Recreation combined to recreate the fort and tell the full story of the Seminole Wars and frontier life in the 19th century, with the help of a small museum, video presentation, Seminole artifacts, and restored historical homes.

Christmas itself thrives on seasonal gags, with streets named for Santa's reindeer, a post office with a mail slot just for Santa, and a full-time Christmas tree and nativity scene. Most visitors want to know how the place got its name, though, and it has nothing to do with elves or reindeer. Back in 1837, as there were no obvious landmarks to pin the fort's name to, it was named for the day Eustis' men arrived. Which was, of course, December 25.

Address 1300 N Fort Christmas Road, Christmas, FL 32709, +1 (407) 254-9310, www.ocfl.net/CultureParks/Parks.aspx | **Getting there** By car, take the East-West Expressway (SR-408) all the way east to its terminus at E Colonial Drive, then take E Colonial 11 miles east to N Fort Christmas Road. Turn left and the park is on the left. | **Hours** Daily 9am – 4pm | **Tip** Don't leave Christmas without visiting Swampy, the 200-foot gator, which is actually the front building of clever Jungle Adventures animal park (26205 E Colonial Drive, Christmas, www.jungleadventures.com).

30 Garden Theatre

Winter Garden's comeback kid

The first movie theater in Central Florida built for the new-fangled "talking pictures," the Garden Theatre in the heart of Winter Garden has seen a roller-coaster history of boom and bust. The booms have been particularly resounding, and the busts have produced their share of misery. For 26 years, it suffered through a cultural wasteland, while it was left in the dark, ignored and practically derelict, plus the ignominy of being used as a tractor supply store. Luckily, this period gem was lovingly restored and re-opened in 2008 to become a local community treasure that now contributes more than $3 million annually to the Orlando economy.

The theater opened its doors in 1935 at the height of the movie phenomenon sweeping the US. Its striking Mediterranean Revival architecture, topped with a tiled roof, was matched by a unique interior modeled after a Spanish courtyard, featuring cute "Romeo & Juliet" balconies and a dark blue, star-studded ceiling. In the 1950s, it continued to be Winter Garden's prime entertainment source, but its popularity was waning, thanks to the nation's growing fixation with television.

By 1963, the writing was on the wall: there was no future for single-screen cinemas. The owners shut it down later that year, and it languished, largely forgotten in a town struggling for an identity in the modern shopping mall landscape. For a while, it was an adjunct to the neighboring Hounds Motor Co., with its gorgeous interior disfigured by tractor storage and repairs.

Happily, the city bought the site in 2002 and, in partnership with Winter Garden's Heritage Foundation, painstakingly restored the interiors and used it as a key element in the revitalization of the historic downtown area. Now a live-performance theater, it again thrives on local patronage and community support amid a vibrant urban rebirth, a comeback story for the ages.

Address 160 W Plant Street, Winter Garden, FL 34787, +1 (407) 877-4736, www.gardentheatre.org | **Getting there** By car, take the East-West Expressway (SR-408) west to the Florida Turnpike. Take the Turnpike one exit to Highway 429, and then Highway 429 one junction to exit 24 to Plant Street. Turn left on Plant Street and continue for two miles. The Theatre is on the left. | **Hours** See website for showtimes | **Tip** The Winter Park Playhouse stages high-quality musicals in an intimate setting and also offers a community outreach program for children (711 N Orange Avenue, Winter Park, www.winterparkplayhouse.org).

31 Gertrude's Walk

How a pretty woman's pride got railroaded

Legend has it that Gertrude Sweet was "the prettiest woman in Orange County" in the 1880s. That level of admiration inspired her brother Charles, who happened to be the mayor and city surveyor, to name a major downtown street after her. But Charles Sweet's sweet gesture would turn positively sour. While details of his seemingly generous gift to his sibling are sparse, what happened soon after was enough to make poor Gertrude feel well and truly disrespected and disappointed.

Gertrude Avenue was briefly the city's widest street until the South Florida Railroad purchased the land for its narrow-gauge track that extended from Sanford to Orlando, in 1880, and used the thoroughfare for its main line. Gertrude Avenue became Gertrude's sidewalk, demoted from the ranks of grand avenue to a short stretch fit only for walking and bicycling.

A hundred years later, the semi-obscured, three-block trail (0.25 miles) that runs between W Church Street and W Washington Street was commemorated in her honor as part of a beautification project, adding a link to the Orlando Urban Trail in the process. Look for weathered bronze plaques featuring the relief of Gertrude herself holding an umbrella, and a second sign below it that reads, *Gertrude's Walk.* The plaques are attached to the brick walls running parallel to the railroad tracks. You'll find one at each of the pathway's entry/exit points at W Church Street, W Central Boulevard, W Pine Street, and W Washington Street.

In May, 2014, the railroad found new life as the SunRail commuter railway service.

However, all was not lost for lovely Gertrude. In a nod to her avenue's former glory, Gertrude's Walk transitions into N Gertrude Avenue at its intersection with W Washington Street. It was shown some love in October, 2022 with a major clean-up and new, pollinator-friendly landscaping after Hurricane Ian blew through.

Address To the right of 123 W Church Street, Orlando, FL 32802 | Getting there SunRail to Church Street; bus 60 to S Orange Avenue & E Church Street | Hours Unrestricted | Tip Enjoy all or part of the 20-mile, semi-secluded West Orange Trail by bike or on foot, starting in Winter Garden and heading as far north as Apopka (17914 FL-438, Winter Garden, www.ocfl.net).

32 Get Up And Go Kayaking

Paddling amid a nighttime glow

Much like love itself, Get Up And Go Kayaking's after-dark tour is mostly in the dark, surrounded by a brilliant glow, and teamwork is required to make the experience worthwhile. Paddling along Winter Park's Chain of Lakes via Venetian-style canals, couples will view the hidden beauty beneath the water through the bottom of their clear, light-up, tandem kayak during a "Glow in the Dark" nighttime tour. For an intimate date night, this one will be far less predictable and far more memorable than dinner and a movie.

Justin and Tia Buzzi understand how profound a fantastic date can be. They were still dating when the idea of owning a clear kayaking venture took its first steps toward reality in 2016. Within the year, they launched at three sites: Titusville for spectacular bioluminescent tours; Rock Springs, where the water is crystal-clear; and Winter Park, which Tia took ownership of after graduating from the University of Central Florida. All good relationships take work, but this couple was no stranger to hands-on labor, having assembled kayaks in their apartment and scouted out the best waterways for their tours in the early days. By 2018, the business was so successful it expanded to franchise opportunities.

The two-hour Glow in the Dark tours are almost transcendentally beautiful, offering a serene experience while gliding across the lakes and canals illuminated by your two-person kayak's glowing LED lights. The canal passes behind Winter Park homes, with lush, semi-tropical foliage lining the banks, while Lake Virginia, Lake Osceola, and Lake Maitland's aquatic plants can be seen through the bottom of your kayak. If you're lucky, you might catch sight of bass, catfish, sunfish, or gar.

Not quite ready to commit to the full-on romance of a Glow in the Dark tour? Get Up And Go Kayaking also offers invigorating daytime tours and sunset tours.

Address 410 Ollie Avenue, Winter Park, FL 32789, +1 (407) 212-7306, www.getupandgokayaking.com/locations/winter-park | Getting there Bus 443 to Osceola & Ollie Avenues | Hours Daily 8am–5pm, see website for tour times | Tip For a relaxed tour past mansions and Floridian flora, take a 50-minute ride along Winter Park Chain of Lakes with Scenic Boat Tours (312 E Morse Boulevard, Winter Park, www.scenicboattours.com).

33__Give Kids The World Village

Where wishes really do come true

Give Kids The World Village not only encourages eating ice cream for breakfast, but they also strive to make sure every "wish" – including a sweet start to each day – is met with a resounding "Yes!" This non-profit resort dedicated to giving children with life-threatening illnesses and their families a cost-free, one-week break from the stress of medical concerns is Orlando's most beloved charity. But most people don't know they can volunteer at the Village, doing joyful jobs that include serving up ice cream for breakfast.

Give Kids The World was started in 1986 by hotelier, lifelong philanthropist, and holocaust survivor Henri Landwirth, and over the years it has made the wishes come true for children from 76 countries and across the US. In 1989, Landwirth opened the Village, a place where families can focus on nothing but fun, from the time they wake up in their fantasy villa to the time they close their eyes after each day's adventure.

Volunteers are the magic that makes the village work, from passing out popcorn on movie night to greeting families at the airport, or helping create a winter wonderland festival. Walt Disney World, Universal Orlando, and SeaWorld are among the Village's major sponsors. Their famous characters stop by often for meet-and-greets, while Halloween, holiday season with Santa, and a birthday party for village mascot Mayor Clayton are celebrated each week so that every guest has a chance to experience them. These events, plus food service, ride operations, kid-friendly spa treatments, and much more all have roles the public can play. Kids as young as 10 can fill certain positions (with an adult), and volunteers' time at the Village will truly leave them with some of the most magical memories Orlando has to offer.

Address 210 S Bass Road, Kissimmee, FL 34746, +1 (407) 396-1114, www.gktw.org | Getting there By car, from I-4 W take exit 64 and stay left for east FL-192. Continue to Bass Road and turn right. The destination is on the right. | Hours Vary by volunteer position; see website | Tip Take volunteerism to the streets by pitching in and cleaning the city up with non-profit organization Keep Orlando Beautiful. Volunteers all meet in one location and then go out into the city in groups (1010 S Woods Avenue, www.orlando.gov).

34__ *Global Convergence*
Orlando's fishy artwork

"What's with all the fish?" It's a commonly heard query in downtown Orlando on the corner of Heritage Square Park at the junction of Central Boulevard and Magnolia Avenue, where a vivid, 12-foot-high, blue-and-silver sphere sits in splendid isolation. On close inspection, the aluminum globe – like a giant bracelet charm – is absolutely full of fish – shoal bass, to be precise. The luminous structure clearly has a story to tell.

The 2013 structure is by Alabama artist Deedee Morrison, and it is part of the downtown See Art Orlando project of nine permanent, contemporary sculptures designed to improve the aesthetic and cultural image of the city, which also includes the striking *The Muse of Discovery* in Lake Eola Park. Morrison's work *Global Convergence* is a dual message of the diversity of our planet and its ever-greater interconnections via technology, infrastructure, and lifestyle; hence the globe itself. The fish represent Nature and the vital need for humanity to exist in harmony with it on a global scale.

The technology used to construct the sculpture is impressive – laser-cut panels of industrial grade, powder-coated aluminum set over a cobalt interior – but the sense of life from the shoal of fish seemingly swimming in its depths is remarkable. The bass were printed on the panels with the traditional Japanese print-making technique of Gyotaku, using sumi ink and rice paper, and the life-sized impressions needed only the finishing touch of their eyes by hand. Attention-grabbing during the day, *Global Convergence* is even more conspicuous after dark, when the LED lighting comes into its own with 12 nightly light shows in shades of blue. This extra dimension simulates the four seasons in the region's freshwater system and highlights 31 Florida fish species that are rare, threatened, or endangered in the convergence of humanity and the natural world.

Address Heritage Square Park, 65 E Central Boulevard, Orlando, FL 32801, +1 (407) 246-2121, www.orlando.gov | **Getting there** Bus 60 to N Magnolia Avenue & E Central Boulevard | **Hours** Unrestricted | **Tip** Take advantage of the full, online walking guide of the See Art Orlando sculptures, six of which can be found in Lake Eola Park (512 E Washington Street, www.orlando.gov/Our-Government/Departments-Offices/Venues/See-Art-Orlando).

35 Greenwood Cemetery
The ghosts of Baby Land

Far too many headstones in downtown Orlando's Greenwood Cemetery are tiny. Grouped together in three numbered sections under the general title, Baby Land, they mark the resting place of infants and children who departed life too soon. Many of these deaths occurred on the day the child was born, or they indicate a stillbirth, as evidenced by the single date on their headstones signifying both the beginning and the tragic end of their lives. The stark emptiness of some markers reveals infants who passed without having been given a name.

Others here died under the "care" of the now-pejoratively named Sunland Training Center for Retarded Children, which was formerly located just 12 miles away. Orlando's Sunland facility was a place where children with severe mental and physical challenges were housed and treated, but due to its appalling conditions and the suspected medical abuse of its patients, a class action lawsuit against the State of Florida was filed in 1979. It took another six years before the center was shuttered, one year after the 1984 passing of the Developmental Disabilities Assistance and Bill of Rights Act.

Prominent Orlando residents are also buried in Greenwood Cemetery, including Bob Carr, for whom the Bob Carr Performing Arts Center is named; Captain James Parramore, whose surname lives on as Orlando's Parramore district; dairy mogul T. J. Lee; and Joseph Bumby, namesake of Bumby Avenue.

But it's the utterly heart-wrenching collection of Baby Land graves that holds a paranormal fascination. Amid the solemn quiet of their grassy resting places, the laughter of ghostly children and the tinkling tunes of a music box are said to be heard. Some small souls never made it that far. Visitors who wander the playground that sits on the site of the former Sunland Training Center may feel the gentle pull of a child's hand on their clothing.

Address 1603 Greenwood Street, Orlando, FL 32801, +1 (407) 246-2616, www.orlando.gov, greenwood@orlando.gov | Getting there By car, take the East-West Expressway (SR-408) east to Exit 11B to E Anderson Street. Turn right on S Mills Avenue then turn left on Greenwood Street. | Hours Mon–Fri 8am–4pm | Tip Fifteen-year-old Colleen Osborne also died too young, the suspected victim of serial killer Christopher Wilder. She rests in the Garden of Remembrance next to Chapel Hill Cemetery (8405 Trevarthon Road).

36__Hamburger Mary's
The haunted hamburger joint

Whether it's Marys & Mimosas, Dining with the Divas, or Saturday Cabaret Dinner Show, there is always something special happening at Hamburger Mary's Bar & Grille in the heart of downtown. The nightly drag shows – along with creative cocktails – are perennially popular and a beacon of the local gay community. But those who are supernaturally attuned insist that is not all you're likely to see at Mary's. The historic location in the former Church Street Station is said to be haunted by a variety of lively spirits from yesteryear.

These hauntings are not surprising, considering the location. Before it was a popular hamburger joint, it was a key part of Orlando's 19th-century railroad station. Built as a hardware store and warehouse by British entrepreneur Joseph Bumby, it became the ticket office of the South Florida Railroad when the line reached the city in 1882. The imposing Victorian red brick structure was completed in 1886 and the Bumby family became Orlando's hardware barons for the next 80 years. In 1972, Bob Snow and his grand entertainment project arrived in Church Street and the Bumby Building was transformed into the Buffalo Trading Company, a Western-themed clothing store. The piecemeal closing of Church Street Station saw the building briefly become Toojay's Deli before Mary's brought its San Francisco-based drag entertainment to downtown in 2008.

And, ever since it opened its doors, reports of the apparition of a young girl in Victorian dress appearing either at the restaurant's windows or skipping gaily along the street outside have been numerous, while others tell of spectral bartenders, busily wiping down counters and smiling at customers. So much so, the city's several ghost tours make a particular point of highlighting Church Street and the happy Bumby haunts, while they are also recorded in a document at the Orange County History Regional Center.

Address 110 W Church Street, Orlando, FL 32801, +1 (321) 319-0600, www.hamburgermarys.com/orlando | **Getting there** SunRail to Church Street; bus 60 to S Orange Avenue & W Church Street | **Hours** Tue & Thu 11am–9pm, Wed & Sun 11am–4pm, Fri & Sat 11am–10pm | **Tip** A proposed restaurant across the street became a "haunted" legal case in 2005 when the owners were sued for pulling out of their lease, claiming the building had ghosts. Keep your eye out to see what kind of business moves into the space (123 E Church Street).

37 Hannibal Square Heritage Center

The soul of an African American community

The Hannibal Square Heritage Center is a legacy project in the heart of Winter Park's West Side established by the Crealdé School of Art in 2007 as a tribute to Hannibal Square's Black community, some freed after the Civil War, whose labor built the town once occupied by wealthy, white socialites and industrialists. Residents tell their individual stories in framed, black-and-white photographs from the area's early days, combined with their personal reminiscence and a current photograph.

Among the stories are those of the first Black student to attend Winter Park High School post-segregation; a local whose property was swallowed up by a sinkhole; a family's sugar cane press used to make syrup that could be bartered or sold; a patriarch born into slavery before becoming one of Winter Park's first Black residents; and Minnie, a prized mule who inherited her name from the family's two previous mules, both called Minnie.

The museum's second floor acts as a showcase for today's Black artists through limited-time exhibitions such as heritage quilts, folk art, and a tribute to the town of Eatonville, the USA's first incorporated African American municipality.

Outside, you'll find a Memory Wall made by folk artist Mr. Imagination, a.k.a. Gregory Warmack, who uses "found" and salvaged objects to create his pieces. In this instance, he invited passers-by to leave items with him during the week he worked on the project. He then surrounded the "angel" figures he built into the wall with the donated trinkets. Look for a hair straightener from the local beauty parlor, rusty keys, a railroad spike, and small plastic toys contributed by children. A chicken bone from a random stranger has since fallen out, but its impression remains.

Address 642 W New England Avenue, Winter Park, FL 32789, +1 (407) 539-2680, www.hannibalsquareheritagecenter.org | **Getting there** Bus 9, 23 to S Denning Drive & Douglas Avenue | **Hours** Wed & Thu noon–4pm, Fri noon–5pm, Sat 10am–2pm | **Tip** Prayer Mission of God in Christ Church was placed on Winter Park's Register of Historic Places for its first pastor's dedication to civil rights and inclusiveness (821 W Lyman Avenue, Winter Park).

38_Harry P. Leu Gardens

Orlando's botanical oasis

The back-story of Orlando could easily be told purely through the many philanthropists and patrons who have left extremely generous donations of land, legacies, and resources to the city over more than 100 years. This story is certainly true when it comes to the floral treasure of Leu Gardens.

Harry P. Leu was born in Orlando in 1884 and quickly became one of its most notable 20th-century citizens. He created one of the largest industrial supply companies in Florida and, together with his wife Mary Jane, bought the 60-acre private estate on Lake Rowena in 1936 that included the original mansion-esque 1888 Colonial home. As avid travelers, the couple habitually brought back seeds and plants from trips abroad, especially roses, camellias, and azaleas. Over the course of 25 years, they created a remarkable, private, botanical wonderland.

In an admirable gesture of generosity, the Leus deeded most of the estate to the city in 1961 for a mere $58,018.73, though its value was more than $1 million, on the understanding it would become a perpetual garden showcase for the general public.

Visitors were initially invited to "Relive Orlando's Past" for the grand sum of $1. The fully restored Leu House was listed on the National Register of Historic Places, and the lush, tropical gardens proclaimed "miles of scenic walkways through forests of camellias and avenues of giant camphors." Today, the beautifully tranquil site boasts more than 15,000 plants in 12 artfully themed sections, including herb and vegetable gardens, a rose garden, camellias, and cycads, plus a glorious gazebo that is a popular spot for wedding ceremonies. Also look for a series of sculptures and a huge floral clock, as well as the family cemetery of the Mizell family, the first owners, notably the 1870 grave of David Mizell, the only sheriff of Orlando to be killed in the line of duty.

Address 1920 N Forest Avenue, Orlando, FL 32803, +1 (407) 246-2620, www.leugardens.org | Getting there Bus 6 to Corrine Drive & N Bumby Avenue; by car, from I-4 E take exit 85 and turn right on Princeton Street. Then turn right on N Mills Avenue, left on Nebraska Street, and left on Corrine Drive and then take the first left into the main entrance. | Hours Mon–Wed & Fri–Sun 9am–5pm, Thu 9am–8pm | Tip Nearby Mead Garden has free admission to its 47 acres of natural habitat, trails, boardwalk, a butterfly garden, and more (1300 S Denning Drive, Winter Park, www.meadgarden.org).

39 Holocaust Memorial and Education Resource Center

Step behind the world's most famous bookcase

Orlando's Holocaust Memorial and Education Resource Center in Maitland expanded its reach as far as the Anne Frank House in Amsterdam when it added a virtual reality experience to its permanent exhibits. *Behind the Bookcase: The Secret Annex through Anne's Eyes* allows visitors the rare opportunity to "walk" around the concealed annex where Anne Frank and her family hid from the Nazis from July 1942 until August 1944, through the use of VR Oculus goggles. It was there that Anne wrote in her touching and insightful diary, and the VR experience captures the rooms as they were before eight people hiding in the annex – the Franks, the Van Pels family, and Fritz Pfeffer – were betrayed, arrested, and sent to concentration camps. None but Anne's father Otto survived.

The tour begins with an introduction that provides historical context before viewers are taken behind the bookcase that hid the "secret annex." You'll experience two small living areas and a bathroom used by the Franks on the left, and a steep stairwell leading to the upstairs annex just beyond the entry door. At the top, viewers walk into a kitchen and common area, as well as the Van Pels' bedroom, with a small room just beyond for Peter Van Pels. A ladder leads to the storage attic.

Viewers sit in swivel chairs to make the VR's 360-degree turning range feel more "natural," and ambient sounds can be heard in each room. The narrator speaks as the voice of Anne Frank to describe what you are seeing through excerpts from her diary. Look for icon indicators throughout the tour, including a hand that triggers movement of an item, footprints that show you where to "walk," a magnifying glass that allows you to see something up-close. This technology gives us an emotional look inside one of history's most tragic eras.

Address 851 N Maitland Avenue, Maitland, FL 32751, +1 (407) 628-0555, www.holocaustedu.org | Getting there SunRail to Maitland; by car, from I-4 E take exit 90 A-B to exit 90 A to reach Maitland Boulevard. Continue for one mile to N Maitland Avenue and turn right. The center is on the right. | Hours Tue–Thu 10am–4pm, Fri 10am–1pm, Sat & Sun noon–4pm | Tip Jewish comfort food takes center stage at Deli Desires, from crisp bialys to whitefish sandwiches and Dr. Brown's soda (715 Fern Creek Avenue, Suite B, www.delidesires.com).

40___iFly Orlando
Indoor skydiving anyone can do

Skydiving is a bucket-list experience for many, but the risks of departing an airplane and heading Earth-ward at 120 miles per hour are a daunting prospect. iFly Orlando's indoor skydiving wind tunnels pose no such threat. Even novices and children can experience the thrill of freefalling – without the danger.

Feeling the wind rushing past you as your body floats on a massive wall of air is unforgettable. It's all down to four massive fans at the top of the building that blow downward from inside the walls and then upward through the transparent, vertical tunnel, creating an upsurge as the air blasts through a metal mesh floor. But you won't notice that feat of engineering as you hover several feet in the air while an instructor gives you pre-arranged hand signals for movements that will enhance your flight. Want to know what it feels like to bounce gently off the mesh floor? You'll probably do that a few times while learning to fly. Want to do tricks? Your instructor can help you figure out how, with just small, simple movements. The basics of indoor skydiving are easy enough that kids as young as three can safely experience this thrilling adventure.

Each flight starts with an instruction session before flyers get fitted out in special jumpsuits, helmets, and goggles, plus foam earplugs to help dampen the noise from the fans. Then it's off to the tunnel for the ride of a lifetime!

Those who prefer to keep their feet firmly planted can just sit and enjoy watching others "fly." Professional skydivers use the tunnels for practice too. That's one of the great features at iFly Orlando because these pros can perform aerial movements that seem to break every law of physics as they flip, cartwheel, spin, and do mid-air head stands. You can happily be a spectator. With such compelling entertainment, you'll be tempted to break out the popcorn and stay awhile!

Address 8969 International Drive, Orlando, FL 32819, +1 (407) 337-4359, www.iflyworld.com/orlando | Getting there Bus 8, 38, 42 to International Drive & Samoan Court | Hours Mon–Thu 11am–8pm, Fri 11am–8:30pm, Sat 9am–9pm, Sun 10am–8pm | Tip Love extreme sports? Try themed indoor and outdoor paintball games with Orlando Paintball, including SWAT vs Convicts, Aliens, and Nuclear Meltdown (7215 Rose Avenue, www.orlandopaintball.com).

41 Jack Kerouac House

The famous "lost" home

How could a famous writer's home become forgotten? You'd think something like that would be well-known, especially when the writer in question was an icon of the 1950s Beat Generation. Yet for decades, the house where Jack Kerouac lived and wrote *The Dharma Bums* (the follow-up novel to his era-defining *On The Road*) was lost from the College Park district. Local folklore knew Kerouac had been the modest neighborhood's most famous resident, but exactly where was lost to memory. Until a dogged TV reporter got on the trail in 1996.

Bob Kealing worked for Orlando's NBC affiliate, and the mystery piqued his curiosity to such an extent he made it his mission to locate the "lost" home. After several months of diligent investigation, Kealing tracked it down to the ramshackle, one-bed duplex at 1418 ½ Clouser Avenue, a 1920s Sears, Roebuck and Co. kit house in urgent need of repair. His report on the rundown building in turn roused local bookshop owners Marty and Jan Cummins, who created a unique vision for the house. Teaming up with the Emmy Award-winning Kealing and others in the community, they were able to buy the house, embark on extensive renovations, and establish a living legacy to Kerouac's heritage.

Today, it's home to the Kerouac Project, a writer residency program that invites budding authors to spend three months at a time working on their craft in the very room where Kerouac wrote *The Dharma Bums* in just 12 days in 1957, cementing his position, according to *The New York Times*, as the voice of the new, young generation – an accolade that ultimately proved his undoing. Kerouac lived in Orlando for only a few years before his restless spirit moved him along, ultimately to an early death in St. Petersburg, Florida, in 1969, but the house earned a spot on the National Register of Historic Places in 2016 and remains open to the public on special occasions.

Address 1418 Clouser Avenue, Orlando, FL 32804, www.kerouacproject.org | **Getting there** By car, from I-4 E take exit 84B for E Colonial Drive. Turn left onto Colonial Drive, then right onto Edgewater Drive, left onto Golfview Street, and right onto Clouser Avenue. | **Hours** Unrestricted from outside only; see website for event schedule | **Tip** Also in College Park, the unusual 1940 William Doerr House is one of the few surviving models of Orlando art moderne architecture and a city Historic Landmark (324 DeSoto Circle, www.orlando.gov).

42 John Mott Marker

Lake Eola's Nobel Peace Prize

You'd think a city would treasure its doers and achievers, its award-winners and community heroes. True, Orlando does celebrate notables like Dr. Philip Phillips, Reverend Mary Augusta Safford, and Zora Neale Hurston, but somehow John Mott, Nobel Prize recipient, slipped through the cracks. Or, at least, his house did.

John Raleigh Mott came to Orlando relatively late in life after a stellar career as a leader in the world Christian movement. A tireless organizer, mentor, and champion of race relations, he retired to Lake Eola in 1938 with a reputation as a peacenik long before the term was coined in the 1960s. He picked up honorary degrees from six universities and was a prime mover in the YMCA and World Student Christian Federation. He would go on to found the World Council of Churches in 1948. The Nobel Peace Prize came his way in 1946, jointly with Emily Greene Balch, for "contributing to the creation of a peace-promoting religious brotherhood across national boundaries."

His modesty almost certainly saved his life in 1912, when he was offered transatlantic passage on a high-profile new ship. He declined, as the voyage was "too fancy" for his tastes. The *Titanic*, of course, sank with major loss of life. And Mott went on to save countless lives during both World Wars in relief work for prisoners of war. So, you'd think his house on E Washington Street – its Nobel Peace Prize taking pride of place – would have been sacrosanct, a timeless reminder of a life well lived. But instead, it was one of three homes bulldozed to make way for a Lake Eola Park expansion in 2013. Today, you will find only a solitary marker that details his extraordinary life and achievements, which included more than 100 Atlantic crossings and 14 of the Pacific. Mind you, his dying wish was that people remember him not for his awards but simply as an evangelist. A lesson to us all.

Address 528 E Washington Street, Orlando, FL 32801 | **Getting there** Bus 62 to E Central Boulevard & S Summerlin Avenue | **Hours** Unrestricted | **Tip** If you visit on a Sunday, stay for the adjacent Orlando Farmers' Market from 10am–3pm, where a wide range of stalls offer fresh produce, arts, and crafts (E Central Boulevard and N Eola Drive, www.orlandofarmersmarket.com).

JOHN R. MOTT HOUSE SITE

Built in 1920, the former house at 528 E. Washington Street was once home to Nobel Peace Prize winner John Raleigh Mott (1869-1955). As general secretary of the National War Work Council, a World War I era Young Men's Christian Association (YMCA) program, Mott received the Distinguished Service Medal for his relief work for prisoners of war. Mott served as general secretary of the YMCA International Committee from 1915-1928 and president of the YMCA World Committee from 1926-1937. As a leader of many civic and Christian organizations, he traveled abroad and delivered thousands of speeches. He averaged 34 days a year on the ocean for 50 years and crossed the Atlantic over 100 times and the Pacific 14 times. Known to travel plainly, he refused a ticket on the Titanic to sail instead on a less extravagant ship. Mott received honorary degrees from six universities including Yale, Edinburgh, Princeton, and Brown. His numerous international honors, awards, and designations included recognition from China, Czechoslovakia, Finland, France, Greece, Hungary, Italy, Japan, Poland, Portugal, Siam, Sweden, and the United States. Mott was awarded the Nobel Peace Prize in 1946 for his humanitarian work.
(Continued on other side)

A FLORIDA HERITAGE SITE
SPONSORED BY THE OSCAR J. NOLLET FAMILY, COMMISSIONER PATTY SHEEHAN,
THE VAN DUSEN-WHEELER FAMILY,
AND THE FLORIDA DEPARTMENT OF STATE

F-952   2016

43 Kelly Park

Orlando's swimming hole

Old-fashioned swimming holes don't come any more charming or authentic than the one at Kelly Park. Tucked away in the greater extent of Rock Springs Run State Reserve, this 355-acre, pristine stretch of semi-tropical forest lies just 30 miles from downtown Orlando. Unlike most Florida springs, this one doesn't bubble up from underground. It gushes from a cave at the foot of a limestone cliff set deep into the forest, pushing 26,000 gallons a minute into the headwaters of Rock Springs Run, one of two tributaries of the Wekiva River. This river is one of only two officially designated National Wild and Scenic Rivers in the state.

From the cave's rock pool, swimmers, tubers, and snorkelers float gently downstream through the crystal-clear, 68-degree waters that rarely deepen to more than a few feet, collecting in two freeform pools with stepped entries and a sandy beach. The river then passes out of the park into the State Reserve, and kayak rentals and tours are available at Kings Landing just under a mile to the North. Fish, turtles, and the occasional river otter can usually be seen along the way, along with a wide variety of birdlife and white-tail deer on land.

Kelly Park's little corner of this extensive natural paradise also features a two-and-three-quarter mile hiking loop, picnic sites, a children's playground, and campsites to go with its swimming and tubing attractions. You'll also find a concessions kiosk and well-maintained restrooms to service visitors on weekends and throughout the summer. Campsites range from 35 to 70 feet in length and are sprinkled among the pristine pine forest. Visitors are advised to arrive early in summer, as the park often reaches the 280-vehicle limit soon after its 8am opening (cars line up well in advance). There is a strict no pets and no alcohol policy, and it pays to be bear and alligator aware, like much of Florida.

Address 400 E Kelly Park Road, Apopka, FL 32712, +1 (407) 254-1902, www.ocfl.net/ CultureParks/Parks.aspx | Getting there By car, from I-4 E take exit 94 and turn left on W State Road 434. Turn right onto Wekiva Springs Road for almost five miles and then turn right onto E Welch Road and right onto Rock Springs Road. Continue 3.5 miles and then turn right onto E Kelly Park Road and take the first left into the park. | Hours Summer daily 8am–8pm, winter daily 8am–6pm | Tip You can rent your all-important inner tubes at Rock Springs Bar & Grill just outside the park (4939 Rock Springs Road, Apopka, www.facebook.com/WorldFamousRockSpringsBar).

44 Kress Building

Art Deco in downtown

While Miami scores the lion's share of Art Deco architecture in Florida, Orlando has its shining examples of the eye-catching style, too. Examples include the boutique Wellborn Hotel in Lake Lucerne, a pair of buildings in the Lake Copeland historical district, Washburn Imports, the former Cameo Theater on E Colonial Avenue, and six small 1940s homes in Lake Davis. And then there's the striking Kress Building on Church Street and Orange Avenue.

While it's not quite equal to New York's Art Deco masterpiece of the Chrysler Building, the four-story S. H. Kress department store was a stunning monument in the heart of downtown when it opened in 1935. The five-and-dime empire of pioneering businessman Samuel Henry Kress (1863–1955) was established in 1896, spreading to more than 200 locations throughout the country and becoming a Main Street staple. Despite its blue-collar shopping image, each Kress store was calculated to impress and be aesthetically pleasing and, in the 1930s, that meant lots of Art Deco design. The company's chief architect Edward F. Sibbert (1889–1982) was the man behind the design. When it came to the Kress store in Orlando, he wanted to acknowledge its semi-tropical location as well as infuse it with his personal take on Deco ornamentation.

The Kress store closed in 1981, but the façade has been extremely well-maintained. It features granite veneers and distinctive polychromed terracotta details and inlays with a peculiar design above the original windows on the second and fourth floors. Look closely at the patterns – could those be stylized parrots? You bet! Popular belief says one line of parrots is flying down while the other flies up, but you can be the judge. Here's another peculiarity – the frontage on Church Street (now home to upscale restaurant Kres Chophouse and architects Butler Moore) is a full story taller than its side facing Orange Avenue.

Address 17 W Church Street, Orlando, FL 32801 | Getting there Bus 60 to S Orange Avenue & E Church Street | Hours Unrestricted from outside | Tip The Art Deco Wellborn Hotel is part of a three-building collection that includes the city's oldest documented residence, dating back to 1883 (211 N Lucerne Circle E, www.thewellbornorlando.com).

45 Lake Apopka Wildlife Drive

Where gators are guaranteed

One question often asked by visitors and locals alike is this: "Where can I see alligators in the wild?" The sure answer is Lake Apopka Wildlife Drive in the 20,000-acre Lake Apopka North Shore wildlife preserve, just 20 miles north-west of downtown Orlando. The one-way, 11-mile route winds through a captivating landscape of marshes and canals, with portable restrooms, a picnic pavilion at the historic pumphouse, and plenty of animal sightings, including gators of all sizes from the comfort – and safety – of your car.

The nature preserve's signage and audio tour also reveal how Lake Apopka went from a bass-fishing mecca that attracted the likes of Al Capone and Clark Gable, to the most polluted lake in Florida in the 1970s until it became an epic story of rehabilitation and conservation. Fed by a natural spring, the 50,000-acre lake once drew anglers from across the country to its shores. But after decades of abuse starting in the 1940s, the waterway was a choking green mass of muck and algae caused by fertilizer and pesticide runoff from the farms. It had become a "dead" lake.

Between 1988 and 1999, the Saint Johns River Water Management District bought the surrounding farmland, planted native vegetation, and freed up the water flow that had been restricted by levees dug by the farm owners. The management team also removed the phosphorus-loving gizzard shad fish, whose bottom-feeding added to algae blooms. They then reestablished the decimated bass population. These efforts resulted in a wetland ecosystem the Audubon Society has dubbed "a birders' paradise." Bird lovers can indeed spot up to 372 species that make their part-time or year-round home in the marshes. Visitors may also see armadillos and otters, and, if they're incredibly lucky, coyotes, bears, bobcats, and, of course, gators.

Address 2850 Lust Road, Apopka, FL 32703, +1 (386) 329-4404, www.sjrwmd.com/lands/recreation/lake-apopka | Getting there By car, take FL-429 to exit 29, merge onto Ocoee Apopka Road, then turn left on Harmon Road, right on S Binion Road, then left on Lust Road | Hours Fri–Sun 7am–3pm | Tip Stroll the trail along Shingle Creek, headwaters of Florida's other eco-restoration project, the Everglades (13400 Town Loop Boulevard, Orlando, www.sfwmd.gov/recreation-site/shingle-creek).

46 Lake Baldwin Park

Real roaming room for Fido

When it comes to taking Fido for walkies in the city setting, there are often few places where our canine chums can really stretch their legs. Orlando boasts plenty of dog-friendly hotels, restaurants, and shops, including Celebration Town Center, which gets a Five Bones rating on the super-handy BringFido.com website. However, there are fewer bona fide city dog parks where our furry friends are free to roam free.

In fact, in Winter Park, there is only one significant choice where the four-legged members of the family can be off the leash during park hours of 8am to sunset. Happily, it's also a Five Bones choice. Lake Baldwin Park is home to the largest dog park in Central Florida, and by far the biggest part of the 23-acre city facility is totally dedicated to dogs. Apart from the parking lot and the 2.5-mile paved walkway around the lake, local pups are free to explore the vast, open spaces of the rest of the park at their unleashed leisure and revel in the fact they are the only ones who can go swimming here.

Even better, much of the dog park, which is completely fenced in, is covered by an oak canopy that provides plenty of shade. Several wooded trails and a sandy beach offer lots of active adventure for your pups and their friends, while you can kick back under several picnic pavilions with benches, adjacent to handy public restrooms. There are also several washing stations to ensure you can rinse off your playful puppies before taking them home.

There is even a Facebook page called "Friends of Lake Baldwin Park," which is dedicated to the off-leash portion of Baldwin Park and how everyone can get the most out of this unique amenity. There is one thing you must be aware of, though. Dog owners are reminded to respect the occasional period when the waterfront is fenced off due to a high presence of harmful blue-green algae.

Address 2000 S Lakemont Avenue, Winter Park, FL 32792, +1 (407) 599-3397, www.cityofwinterpark.org, recreation@cityofwinterpark.org | Getting there By car, take the East-West Expressway (SR-408) east to exit 12A for Anderson Street. Stay on Anderson and turn left on S Crystal Lake Drive, which becomes Maguire Road. Turn left on Bennett Road, right onto Virginia Drive, left on Common Way Road, and then immediately right on Lakemont Avenue. Follow Lakemont to the park. | Hours Daily 8am–dusk | Tip Take your best friends for lunch after their park romp at nearby Santiago's Bodega, where well-behaved pets are welcome on the outdoor terrace (802 Virginia Drive, Orlando, www.santiagosbodega.com).

47 Lake Eola Ghost Dog

The tale of the vanishing terrier

Formed from a sinkhole that began in the early 1870s, Lake Eola and its centerpiece Linton E. Allen Memorial Fountain have become icons of downtown Orlando. The newly formed lake and its surrounding land were donated to the City of Orlando in 1883, with the proviso that it should be used as a public park. The nearly one-mile sidewalk around the lake has become a place of enjoyment for walkers and joggers as well as a site for concerts and events at the Walt Disney Amphitheater, a weekly farmers' market with arts and crafts stalls, and the family-friendly fun of pedal-powered Swan Boats.

The lake also boasts five species of actual, live swans, some of whose ancestors were relocated and took up residence in 1922 after squabbling with their fellow fowl on nearby Lake Lucerne. While these large and magnificent waterfowl may be the most obvious fauna inhabiting the park, they are far from the most mysterious. That distinction goes to the little brown terrier that reportedly hangs out near the lake's eastern end. He really grabs visitors' attention not only for his playful attitude but also for the fact he disappears when the fawning and admiration stops.

It isn't known whether the happy tail-wagger was a stray or a regular visitor to the lake in his mortal form, or whether he was abandoned near or, some locals speculate, in the lake, but whichever way he ended up at the park, it is said the ethereal canine is perfectly content to join those who are out walking their more Earthly dogs. And while it is entirely possible a gigantic dose of urban legend is at work here, an evening stroll around the lake makes for healthy, enjoyable entertainment. If you're feeling as though luck is on your side, keep your eye out for this paranormal pooch wandering around during the day or as evening sets in, and rest assured that he is as friendly as he is – or was – adorable.

Address 512 E Washington Street, Orlando, FL 32801, +1 (407) 246-4484,
www.orlando.gov | Getting there Bus 51, 125 to E Robinson Street & N Rosalind Avenue |
Hours Daily 6am – 11:59pm | Tip Buy homemade treats and even a doggie birthday cake
for the wonderful dogs in your life at Bark Avenue Bakery (4307 Vineland Road, Suite H4,
www.barkavenuebakery.com).

48__Lakeview Cemetery
The old, gray Bob is dead

Bob is the only resident of Sanford's Lakeview Cemetery who made the trip to his final resting grounds so many times it is said he knew the route by heart. Owned by T. J. Miller, "Old Bob" was the family's horse, whose job it was to transport the Millers around Sanford in their buggy. But he was also pressed into service pulling Mr. Miller's funeral home hearse for 28 years, shuttling the deceased on their one-way trip, until the gallant steed was finally put out to pasture in 1913 to live his remaining days munching grass and soaking up the Florida sun in peace. In 1914, the old gray horse breathed his last, and became Lakeview Cemetery's single non-human burial. His current headstone, a replacement for the vandalized original that simply read, *Bob*, now reads, *Bob. Faithful 28 Years.*

How did the horse, who lived to a rather astonishing 37 years of age, score a headstone in a cemetery that holds the earthly remains of the human beings he carted there after their passing? Mr. Miller was not only Sanford's sole undertaker, but he was also the owner of Lakeview Cemetery. For his nearly-three-decades of faithful service, Old Bob was also honored with his own obituary in the newspaper.

Time marched on even after the clip-clop of Bob's hearse-hauling hooves was silenced, and today Lakeview Cemetery is tucked away behind All Souls Catholic Cemetery, which has grown up around it. Drive through the second entrance on the left side of W 25th Place, at the intersection with Hardy Avenue, and proceed down the paved lane to a section surrounded by a chain link fence. Bob's simple monument, to the left of the white-fenced entrance and next to a lone palm tree, is adorned with an American flag and a bouquet of silk flowers, and it's the only marker that sits outside the fence, as if Miller's faithful friend is welcoming newcomers to their eternal resting place.

BOB

FAITHFUL 28 YEARS

Address 1975 W 25th Place, Sanford, FL 32773 | Getting there By car, from I-4 E take exit 101A and turn right onto H E Thomas Jr. Parkway. Stay right to reach W 25th Place and then turn left onto Hardy Avenue. | Hours Unrestricted | Tip Bob's original gravestone is in the Sanford Museum, along with a tribute to his life and service (520 E 1st Street, Sanford, www.sanfordfl.gov/government/parks-and-recreation/museum).

49 Little Vietnam

A taste of Southeast Asia

Four blocks hum to their own tune at the intersection of Colonial Drive and Mills Avenue in the Mills 50 business district. That tune is distinctly Vietnamese, from food markets to restaurants, jewelry repair, tailors, and other goods and services.

Nicknamed both "Little Vietnam," and "Little Saigon," the neighborhood was established in the 1970s when approximately 1,100 refugees from Southeast Asia landed in Orlando after fleeing the ravages of the war in Vietnam. As with all who leave their homeland for distant shores, these displaced people proceeded to learn the language, find or create meaningful employment, and adopt some of the customs of their new hometown. Over the years, Orange County's Asian American population swelled to more than 71,000 as Korean, Japanese, Thai, Chinese, and Vietnamese immigrants chose to make Central Florida their home, and a convivial balance was struck, blending the American vibe with the district's distinctly Asian culture.

Dong-A Imports at 706 N Mills Avenue is a virtual warehouse of authentic Asian household goods. Try on some martial arts mat shoes, pick up a kimono, update your saké set, and explore the vast selection of home décor, which includes Buddha statues in an enormous range of sizes and materials. Interested in perfecting your cooking skills? Browse through kitchen items, from rice steamers and individual dishware to restaurant-sized woks, the starting point for an authentic meal when combined with Dong-A Supermarket at 816 N Mills Avenue, which seemingly carries every Asian food item imaginable, including frozen snail meat and roasted, salted duck eggs.

Soak up more culinary immersion at the superb Little Saigon Restaurant, where no one will judge you if you make slurping sounds while you enjoy their wonderfully aromatic *pho*, pronounced "fuh" and conveniently listed on the menu as "noodle soup."

Address E Colonial Drive & Mills Avenue, Orlando, FL 32803 | **Getting there** Bus 125 to Mills Avenue N & E Colonial Drive | **Hours** Dong-A Imports: daily 10am–6pm; Dong-A Supermarket: Fri 9am–9pm, Sat–Thu 9am–8pm | **Tip** The Vietnam War Memorial in the Orlando Veterans Memorial Park honors the fallen soldiers from that war (2380 Lake Baldwin Lane, www.orlando.gov).

50 Lucky's Lake Swim

Wild swimming for the stout of heart

Lucky Meisenheimer, MD, has been making the one-kilometer open water swim across Lake Cane since 1989, having purchased his house specifically for that purpose. He then took his passion to the next level by inviting fellow master swimmers and friends to join him in a grueling endeavor he initially called "Aquatica, Enter the Food Chain 1K Swim," which began as a once-weekly crossing of Lake Cane. By 1995, it had become "Lucky's Lake Swim," taking place six days a week, year-round. The event has now attracted tens of thousands of swimmers from more than 60 countries.

A competitive-swimming veteran of 55 years, Lucky earned Masters World Champion titles and was the coach for the Orange County Special Olympics team, helping to launch the first open water swim that is now one of the events at the summer games. Two of his athletes went on to make the Alcatraz swim.

Be aware that Lucky's Lake Swim is meant for competent swimmers and requires a signed waiver. As Meisenheimer's website states, "If you're not scared now, you will be after you read the release." You may see snakes, turtles, or fish. Alligators are unlikely, but, per the Lake FAQs, "you just never know." After your first successful swim, you'll be invited to ring a bell and then add your signature to Lucky's house. His back wall, patio roof, side wall, overhangs, and part of the pump room are already covered, so make your inaugural swim soon!

There is no charge to join the crack-of-dawn plunge, but Safer-Swimmer floatation devices are required for each participant's first 25 swims because no one wants to go back for you if you should fail to complete the round-trip crossing – or fall victim to the Lake Cane Monster, who is probably but not certainly mythical. With a 6:30am start, the swim takes place in the dark. The monster, known as Slimebo, hasn't caused any serious problems. So far.

Address 6645 Lake Cane Drive, Orlando, FL 32819, www.luckyslakeswim.com | Getting there By car, from I-4 W take exit 75A for S Kirkman Road. Continue to Vineland Road and turn left. Turn right onto Lake Cane Road. Lucky's is on the right, and parking is in the front yard. | Hours Mon–Fri 6:30am, Sat 7:45am; see website for holiday and event hours | Tip Just starting your quest toward swimming mastery? Rosen Aquatic & Fitness Center offers group, semi-private, and private lessons (8422 International Drive, www.rosenaquatic.com).

51 Lukas Nursery & Butterfly Encounter

Experience a butterfly's delicate touch

Lepidopterans love Florida, which sounds a whole lot cuter when their Latin name is replaced by their common name, which is "butterflies." And while you'd expect to find native Floridian plants that attract the state's 170 verified local butterfly species at Lukas Nursery, this 4,000-square-foot conservatory filled with the delicate winged creatures comes as a delightful surprise.

Czechoslovakian immigrants Paul and Mary Lukas arrived in Oviedo, Florida in 1911, began farming, and raised six children. They also had a shoe-repair business. Over the years, Paul acquired more land, and his grandchildren eventually took charge of the family businesses. They had expanded to include the sale of eggs and plants, and business was thriving.

During a fishing trip to Costa Rica with family friend and entomologist Mike Rich, third-generation Philip Lukas visited La Paz Waterfall Gardens and became enchanted with its spectacular butterfly garden. Philip and Mike returned home and made their dream of opening a conservatory a reality. What began as a 1,000-square-foot shack quadrupled to the Butterfly Encounter of today.

Unlike most butterfly houses, Lukas' Butterfly Refueling Station allows visitors to feed the winged insects from their fingertips and take selfies with a butterfly on their nose. You'll learn about the life cycle of 23 native species and get expert guidance on creating a butterfly-friendly garden at home. You can even purchase a selection of these local beauties for an outdoor butterfly release within the state of Florida. Tours are fun and informative, especially around the Swallowtail butterfly, whose four defenses in the caterpillar state include stinking, having fake eyespots, looking like bird poop, and having "karate action" when touched.

Address 1909 Slavia Road, Oviedo, FL 32765, +1 (407) 738-4319, www.lukasnursery.com | **Getting there** By car, take FL-417 N to exit 41, stay right to reach Red Bug Lake Road, then turn right onto FL-426, and right onto Slavia Road | **Hours** Daily 9am–4pm | **Tip** The Lukas family and five others settled in the area they called Slavia. They are remembered by a marker at St. Luke's Lutheran Church (2021 W State Road 426, Oviedo, www.sllcs.org).

52 LunaSea Alpaca Farm

Snuggle with a baby alpaca

Lucy Lee Fowler fell in love with the idea of owning an alpaca. Her husband King took some convincing, but the couple eventually purchased a mottled, gray and white Huacaya alpaca named Lolita, bought five acres of land, added three more alpacas at King's insistence, and then added another eight. Over time, Lucy Lee and King learned more about fleece quality and began buying and selling alpacas with that in mind. Neighbors and passers-by who were intrigued by the unusual "pets" inspired the Fowlers to add another branch to their budding enterprise. They dove into agritourism by opening their farm for tours, hosted by King.

The timing of their decision was ideal. The COVID-19 pandemic encouraged people to find outdoor entertainment, and the farm offered plenty of room for social distancing. King's tours were so successful that Lucy Lee was able to leave her day job and devote her full attention to the administration side of the business.

Unlike most alpaca farms around the country, LunaSea allows visitors to enter the nursery pen and hold one of the youngsters, each of whom is named for a theme chosen each year, such as Candy or Classic Rock Bands. It's impossible not to feel joy with a warm, unbelievably soft, baby alpaca, known as a cria, in your arms. The farm also has llamas, chickens, ducks, dogs, and the fanciest geese you'll ever see. While there is an educational element to a visit here, the real benefit is relieving stress, sparking happiness, and healing saddened hearts.

Along with family-friendly tours that include petting and feeding the animals (reservations required; walk-ups only if space is available), visitors can sign up for Painting with Alpacas or Alpaca Yoga. The crias won't jump on your back the way goats do, but they'll instigate all sorts of playful mischief with your belongings while you're trying to achieve a state of Zen.

Address 18810 Lone Dove Lane, Clermont, FL 34715, +1 (352) 223-9457, www.lunaseaalpacafarm.com | **Getting there** By car, take the East-West Expressway (SR-408) west to the Florida Turnpike, heading north. Take exit 278 to N Hancock Road, turn right onto County Road 561A, and right onto Lone Dove Lane. | **Hours** By reservation only | **Tip** For more pet therapy, visit Soul Haven Ranch and de-stress with the hour-long "My Time with a Miniature Horse" grooming experience (196 Tildenville School Road, Winter Garden, www.soulhavenranch.com).

53_Majesty Building

The I-4 eyesore

When your nickname is "The I-4 Eayesore," it's clear you haven't made a good impression on the locals. But that's the sobriquet attached to the ironically named Majesty Building just off Orlando's main highway in Altamonte Springs, which has been under construction for more than two decades. Announced in 1998, it broke ground in 2001. It quickly became a looming monolith on one of Florida's busiest roads, lingering year after year as an 18-story, steel-and-concrete skeleton of less than elegant proportions.

The shell of a building took shape more firmly when it was enclosed in glass in 2006, but the promised conclusion dates continued to pass year by year with immense regularity. It was mocked mercilessly on social media. @MajestyBuilding was a parody account on X (formerly Twitter), created specifically to highlight the ongoing non-opening in the long-running saga, while Florida comedian Rauce Padgett produced a spoof video in its honor.

In reality, the Majesty Building is a continuing project by religious TV station SuperChannel 55, intended to be debt-free and funded primarily by donations; hence its long, drawn-out construction process. Once complete, it will house the full broadcast facility for the channel, plus 200,000 square feet of office space, in addition to retail space in the rotunda and main tower, banquet and convention facilities, a theater venue, and a covered parking garage for 1,000 cars.

When the power was switched on for the first time in June, 2018, SuperChannel president Claud Bowers was interviewed on WFTV, insisting, "It's a very patient community, and it's going to be rewarded by a beautiful building." He added that completion was expected in "eight to twelve months." Six more years passed with no sign of a majestic debut for the tallest building between Orlando and Jacksonville, and no opening date in sight.

Address 123 E Central Parkway, Altamonte Springs, FL 32701, +1 (407) 263-4040,
www.superchannel.com/SuperChannelCentre/MajestyBuildingInformation.aspx | Getting
there By car, from I-4 E, take exit 92 east and turn right onto E Altamonte Drive, left onto
Palm Springs Drive, and left onto E Central Parkway | Hours Unrestricted | Tip Be sure to
take a stroll in lovely nearby Cranes Roost Park, which offers a one-mile circuit, boardwalk and
covered seating (274 Cranes Roost Boulevard, www.altamonte.org/367/Cranes-Roost-Park).

54 Mathers Social Gathering
Cocktails as dapper as the dress code

If this ultra-modern, speakeasy-style bar looks surprisingly like a furniture store from the 1800s, there's a good reason for it. The Phoenix Building, in the heart of downtown Orlando, originally housed a home goods business when it opened in 1882. It cycled through several other incarnations, including a medical business, a carpentry shop, and an electric company, before reopening as a themed speakeasy, Mathers Social Gathering, in 2017.

The antiques-laden cocktail bar on the third floor pays homage to its 19th-century heritage, with hardwood floors, exposed brickwork, oriental rugs, paintings, and period cabinets to offset a contemporary mixology chic. It was the only building around to survive an 1884 fire, and that period in history is the launching point for Mathers' hideaway theme.

Owners and brothers Keith and Romi Mawardi gathered the watering hole's antiques, furnishings, and signs from their private collections, having curated unique items from various vintage shops, all with an eye toward furthering the building's classic yesteryear vibe. Photos lining the walls show the building as it proceeded through various states during its decades-long life, paying special attention to key moments in Orlando's history.

But you're here for the cocktails. Dive into Bathtub Gin, belly up to the timeless Old Fashioned, or risk your senses with a shot of Green Lady Absinthe, a concoction that was once illegal due to its supposed hallucinogenic properties.

Mathers' humorous "House Rules" for guests' apparel and personal conduct code help to maintain the speakeasy's history of a time when dapper dress was all the rage. Itching for a fisticuffs? Take it outside because cocktail-fueled fighting won't be tolerated here. And guests enjoying the laid-back surroundings should comply with the request not to hoot and holler, even if they've imbibed too much giggle water.

Address 30 S Magnolia Avenue, Orlando, FL 32801, +1 (407) 745-1185, www.mathersorlando.com | Getting there Bus 60, 62 to N Magnolia Avenue & E Central Boulevard | Hours Tue–Sat 4pm–2am | Tip Dress to the nines in a vintage outfit rented or purchased from Orlando Vintage Clothing and Costume (1500 Formosa Avenue, Winter Park, www.orlandovintage.com).

55 Maxine's on Shine

Tinkle amid the alien hordes

Having earned its reputation as an eclectic foodie hangout, Maxine's on Shine in downtown Orlando provides guests with stellar dining, live music, and artsy ambiance. But it's the men's restroom that comes as a surprise of galactic proportions. The walls are covered in paintings of aliens, from the terrifying Xenomorph from the movie *Alien* to the benevolent service droid Robbie the Robot from *Forbidden Planet*, and Bugs Bunny's Earth-hating nemesis Marvin the Martian. Also taking starring roles are 1,000-year-old Maz Kanata and 900-year-old Yoda, the alien who needs no introduction, from the *Star Wars* film franchise. Dr. Who takes pride of place on the restroom's door.

So, what's up with that? When Maxine and her two-year-old son moved into her soon-to-be-husband Kirt Earhart's house, she made it clear she would take over the decorating in every room, except for a single bathroom, which Kirt could decorate as he pleased. Over the years, Kirt and his stepson bonded over the youngster's love of science fiction. When the husband-and-wife team purchased a 1947 building in need of a fresh start and transformed it into funky Maxine's on Shine, its namesake once again had free reign over the restaurant's décor, while her husband was allowed to decorate the men's room. The gents' became an homage to the passion he and his stepson shared for Sci-Fi movies and TV. In stepped local artist Bruce Collins, and *voilá!* An alien restroom was born.

Maxine's is the kind of neighborhood place where friends like to linger over cocktails or wine, and so there's an excellent chance gentlemen pay a visit to the loo. Ladies should give a quick knock to make sure it's empty and then pop in for a peek, Instagram photo optional. Inexplicably, the restroom also has evacuation suggestions next to the toilet in case a Floridian hurricane hits: "Grab Beer, Run Like Hell."

Address 337 N Shine Avenue, Orlando, FL 32803, +1 (407) 743-4227, www.maxinesonshine.com | Getting there Bus 51 to E Robinson Street & N Shine Avenue | Hours Dinner: Wed–Sat 5–9pm; brunch: Fri–Sun 10am–3pm | Tip Florida ranks at number two, behind California, for UFO sightings. Lake Apopka is a great spot for stargazing, and you may even spot an extraterrestrial spacecraft (2929 S Binion Road, Apopka).

56 Melao Bakery
The tastes of Puerto Rico

When you long for a tasty *alcapurria*, *pastel*, or *mofongo*, there is only one place in Orlando and Kissimmee to satisfy that craving: Melao Bakery. These signature dishes – yucca or plantain fritters, pork and adobo stuffed plantains, and deep-fried mashed plantains – all hail from Puerto Rico, and if there is one restaurant associated with that island, it is Melao.

It has been this way since 2008, when husband-and-wife team Eduardo Colon and Denisse Torres opened a café in Kissimmee. They discovered a huge demand for all the *alcapurrias* they could make. Now, with more than 100 staff and two restaurants that practically burst at the seams at peak periods, this classic Boricuan eatery has become a hit with all comers, as their reputation for tasty, authentic, and eye-catching cuisine has spread.

However, their success story wasn't all smooth sailing. They ran a bakery in Puerto Rico for many years, but they decided they'd had enough after a fourth robbery in 24 months. They realized they wanted and needed to try their luck in Florida. Initially, Eduardo trained as a truck driver, but the lure of another bakery soon drew them back to the family business. When the ideal location cropped up, they jumped right back in where they had left off in Puerto Rico. In 2015, they opened a second location near the Florida Mall, and their future was assured. It's said that people arriving from the island at Orlando International Airport make their first stop at Melao on what Eduardo calls "the route of tastiness."

They still import their bread flour from Puerto Rico, along with coffee, malt beverages, and signature sodas. But everything else is made from scratch, including a mouthwatering selection of pastries and baked goods, such as *mallorca*s – fluffy, yeasted buns – and guava *cantinflas*, or traditional stuffed sponge cakes, which are very tasty in any language.

Address 2001 Consulate Drive, Orlando, FL 32837, +1 (407) 348-1777, www.melaobakery.com | Getting there Bus 108, 111 to Consulate Drive & S Orange Blossom Trail | Hours Mon–Fri 6am–9pm, Sat & Sun 7am–9pm | Tip For more tastes of the island, try Crocante Restaurant, which also displays Puerto Rican art to go with some fine, authentic food (4311 E Colonial Drive, www.crocantekitchen.com).

57 __ Mennello Museum of American Art
The poignant artistry of Earl Cunningham

That this Smithsonian American Affiliate art museum exists at all is purely down to artistic detective Marilyn Mennello, who "discovered" unknown folk artist Earl Cunningham in 1969. Marilyn happened upon Cunningham's work in his rented St. Augustine curio shop, Over The Fork. The white-haired, 76-year-old fellow had a small studio in a back room.

Cunningham (1893–1977) went out into the world on his own at the age of 13, finding work to support himself, including raising chickens for the federal government during World War II. His evocative American folk-art landscape and seascape paintings were based on his memories of time spent in locations where he'd lived, such as Maine, Michigan, New York, Georgia, and Florida. Each idyllic setting – many of which include a harbor, symbolic of the safe haven that seems to have eluded the artist – is given an imaginative twist through skies and bodies of water in shades of orange, pink, and green. His unusual color palette and somewhat child-like style are the starting point for the complex stories and emotions his works convey.

When Mennello discovered Cunningham's paintings, she and husband Michael made it their mission to bring the artist's work to light. It took time to convince him to sell his pieces, but once he agreed, they purchased as many as they could at $500 per painting. During lunch with Orlando's then-mayor Glenda Hood, Marilyn mentioned the paintings, and the mayor informed her the city owned the former home of Howard Phillips, son of businessman Dr. Phillip Phillips, which was the perfect place to display the artist's work.

In November, 1998, the Mennellos founded the museum, which now includes a wide array of American folk art. Tragically, Cunningham never saw it, having died by suicide in 1977.

Address 900 E Princeton Street, Orlando, FL 32803, +1 (407) 246-4278, www.mennellomuseum.org | **Getting there** Bus 125 to Princeton Street & N Mills Avenue | **Hours** Tue–Sat 10:30am–4:30pm, Sun noon–4:30pm | **Tip** Orlando Family Stage, just across the street from the Mennello, makes the perfect, family-friendly introduction to theatrical performances (1001 E Princeton Street, www.orlandorep.com).

58 Mills 50 Murals
Freddie Mercury's hairy armpit

Floyd's 99 Barbershop in the Mills 50 District advertises cuts, colors, and shaves on their window signage. But they would need an enormous straight razor to handle the massive hairy armpit painted on the side of the building as part of a posthumous tribute to Freddie Mercury, former lead singer for the rock band Queen, and to the neighborhood's LGBTQIA+ community. The frontman's likeness portrays him dressed in a white tank top with a studded, dog-collar-style band around his upper arm, recalling the outfit he wore during Queen's performance in the 16-hour Live Aid "Feed the World" concert at London's Wembley Stadium on July 13, 1985 to raise funds toward famine relief in Africa.

The word "Never" painted above and to the right of the rock star is the last name of the mural's artist Jonas Never, who hails from Los Angeles. One of the founders of the Floyd's 99 Barbershop franchise met Never in a bar in LA and asked the artist to paint his first commissioned mural. He was then commissioned by Kyle and Sarah Sleeth, owners of the N Mills Avenue shop. They considered another image, but because of a revived interest in Queen due to the release of the *Bohemian Rhapsody* movie starring Rami Malek and the barbershop's rock 'n roll style, they landed on Freddie.

Never has since painted sports stars, celebrities, and other pop culture icons around the country, including three murals in the Mills 50 area. The Fairbanks Avenue location of Floyd's 99 Barbershop features a mural by Never of beloved children's television star Fred Rogers, a local boy who made good.

Freddie Mercury is one of 44 murals in Mills 50, which include a version of the "wings" murals that have become Instagram-popular across the country (find it at 912 N Mills Avenue). Many of the murals are Pride-related in support of the 49 individuals killed during the 2016 Pulse Nightclub shooting.

Address 842 N Mills Avenue, Orlando, FL 32803 | Getting there Bus 125 to N Mills Avenue & Illinois Street | Hours Unrestricted | Tip Love street art? Watch for painted traffic signal boxes throughout the Mills 50 District. They're part of Orlando's Art Box Project (various locations, www.mills50.org/art-projects/art-box-project).

59 Monument of States
A vision of national unity

Kissimmee might seem an odd spot for a tribute to national harmony, but the junction of Lakeview Drive and Monument Avenue is testament to a special work of patriotism – and rock collecting. Here, in splendid eccentricity, the colossal 50-foot Monument of States celebrates US unity during World War II. The work of Dr. Charles W. Bressler-Pettis, it was a vision of both unanimity and tourism promotion in a town making a name for itself in the 1940s.

The larger-than-life Harvard Medical School graduate was born in Missouri in 1889 but made Kissimmee his winter home when he wasn't traveling the world. He and his wife covered more than 78,000 miles on a four-year honeymoon through North America, Europe, and Africa, during which he collected rocks from places they visited. In the US, he drove a gold-and-purple Cadillac adorned by a golden lion and the slogan, "Tourist Paradise – Kissy-Me, Florida."

At the outbreak of the war, Bressler-Pettis, who was also President of Kissimmee's All States Tourist Club and a one-man chamber of commerce, aimed to salute the unified spirit of the nation and sought rocks from governors of every state to add to his grand design. President Roosevelt contributed three from his Hyde Park collection. Along with other oddities, including fossils, petrified wood, and even bits of bone, each contribution was worked into concrete slabs and mounted in a towering collection of community spirit, as local donors provided bags of cement. Dedicated in 1943 by Senator Claude Pepper, its 50th anniversary was celebrated with the addition of a time capsule to be opened in 2043.

See if you can spot the two stones on the Monument for "Doc" and wife Laura among several personal adornments. Here's another curiosity: walk around the Monument counterclockwise from the west face and see the topmost words spell out the phrase, "World's Most Unique Monument."

Address 300 E Monument Avenue, Kissimmee, FL 34741 | **Getting there** By car, take I-4 to the Florida Turnpike south to exit 249. Turn right onto E Osceola Parkway, left onto Michigan Avenue, left onto N Main Street; and left onto E Monument Avenue. | **Hours** Unrestricted | **Tip** After visiting the monument, take a stroll along lovely adjacent Lakefront Park, part of the Florida National Scenic Trail (201 Lakeview Drive, www.kissimmee.gov).

60 Morse Museum
The definitive Tiffany collection

Louis Comfort Tiffany (1848–1933) is in the pantheon of American glass artists and a shining example of the Art Nouveau and Aesthetic movements. The largest collection of his work in the world forms the heart of the Charles Hosmer Morse Museum of American Art in Winter Park. The intimate museum showcases a wide range of decorative arts, including 19th-century American pottery and porcelain. But the Tiffany collection is a symphony of classic beauty. The highlight here is a full recreation of his chapel interior originally displayed at the World's Columbian Exposition in Chicago, better known as the 1893 World's Fair.

The Tiffany Chapel was a Byzantine-style masterpiece, with a stunning marble altar as its focal point. The altar almost recedes into the background as you stand at the back of the space. Your eyes are drawn to the story-telling mosaic wall behind it, the vibrant leaded-glass windows on either side of the chapel, and columns completely adorned in mosaic tile. As you get closer, the altar's tesserae – tiny iridescent tiles numbering in the tens of thousands – lend a pillowy softness to the pale marble structure, while gold leaf, mother of pearl, and other delicate details define the design elements. The chapel launched Tiffany as a world-renowned artist.

Over the course of his lifetime, Tiffany worked in several other mediums, including jewelry, leaded-glass lamps, metalwork, paintings, and even furniture, some of which he kept at his Laurelton Hall home in Long Island, New York and now on display at the museum. Don't miss the stunning bouquets of daffodils that top the Carrara marble columns of Laurelton Hall's Daffodil Terrace.

Sadly, the great mansion fell into complete disrepair after Tiffany's death, but these wonderful pieces were saved, and they were then sent to this museum. Also look for his personal letters, photographs, and artistic designs.

Address 445 N Park Avenue, Winter Park, FL 32789, +1 (407) 645-5311, www.morsemuseum.org | Getting there SunRail to Winter Park; by car, from I-4 E take exit 87, turn right onto W Fairbanks Avenue, and left on Park Avenue | Hours Tue–Thu & Sat 9:30am–4pm, Fri 9:30am–8pm, Sun 1–4pm | Tip Experience the powerful form of *Man Carving His Own Destiny* and other works by the sculptor Albin Polasek at his eponymous museum (633 Osceola Avenue, Winter Park, www.polasek.org).

61　Moss Park

Adventures in orienteering

The sport of orienteering is a family-friendly activity that allows children of all ages to take part, and players who are able to read a map and scramble through uneven terrain will enjoy it most. Great exercise both mentally and physically, orienteering originated in Scandinavia in the late 1800s and is based on plotting the quickest route to find a series of specific markers – called "controls" – using only a compass and a map. Don't have a compass? No problem. Moss Park's permanent courses are user-friendly without the aid of a direction finder.

Utilizing the detailed map that features internationally established symbols, orienteers choose their own route via controls based on each course's unique topography, with the goal of finding all the markers on the route. Players record the specific letter or numerical code at each control on a "control card" provided with the orienteering map to prove that they found the marker.

If this is your first time testing your navigational skills, the park's orienteering maps include a traditional legend for all the features found along the trails, such as forested areas that are easy or difficult to navigate, dirt roads, buildings or fences, and areas that are out of bounds, as well as the established symbols of a triangle to indicate the beginning of the course and double circles marking the finish line, plus the single, numbered circles that show where each control marker is located.

You might choose the self-guided Beginners Trail that traverses a well-defined pathway, or opt for the more rugged Advanced Trail, both of which cross landscapes that include marshes, ditches, undergrowth, forested areas, thickets, and open land. Each of these maps has written descriptions of the course elements. Remember to make an online request for a Certificate of Completion for when you've successfully finished your chosen circuit.

Address 12901 Moss Park Road, Orlando, FL 32832, +1 (407) 254-6840,
www.orangecountyfl.net/CultureParks/Parks.aspx | Getting there By car, take the Central
Florida Greeneway southbound to exit 23 go east Moss Park Road. After a half mile, turn
right to stay on Moss Park Road and continue to the park. | Hours See website for seasonal
hours | Tip Orlando Tree Trek Adventure Park is the sky-high ropes course you never
knew you needed, with 97 aerial challenges and two courses for kids (7625 Sinclair Road,
Kissimmee, www.orlandotreetrek.com).

62 Mount Zion Missionary Baptist Church

The Rock of Parramore

Parramore's history is one of racial segregation and deprivation, and that is especially true of its churches. With downtown's Black section effectively split from the rest of the city by the railroad and aptly named Division Street, churchgoers from "the wrong side of the tracks" had to create their own places of worship. With immense fortitude, they created a network of more than 15 churches that chart the district's history.

Foremost among them is Mount Zion Missionary Baptist Church, or the Rock of Parramore, which has served the community since 1880, from its earliest days when Black people were forbidden even to build a church, and members held services in a bush arbor instead. It had multiple addresses until 1956, when, under the leadership of Reverend Nathaniel Staggers, the church broke ground on an ambitious building project for a hefty $250,000. It would be a magnificent brick church in classical Revival style, featuring a columned entrance and a graceful steeple. Funded largely by churchgoers, who also supplied some of the labor, construction was a huge undertaking over seven years. And it firmly established Mt. Zion as a neighborhood treasure, serving as a center for civil rights issues and offering high-energy services. Today, Mount Zion provides a live-streamed Wednesday Bible Study, women's prayer call on Saturday mornings, and the highly musical Sunday Service with charismatic pastor Reverend Dr. Robert Spooney. All visitors are most welcome.

Despite ongoing gentrification, Mount Zion has stayed faithful to its community values under Dr. Spooney, who was born in Parramore and continues to espouse this core tenet: "We are one, our cause is one and, if we are to be successful, we must help one another." Just as it aimed to do in 1880.

Address 535 W Washington Street, Orlando, FL 32810, +1 (407) 423-0023,
www.mtzionmbic.org | Getting there Bus 25, 54 to W Washington Street & N Terry
Avenue | Hours Services Wed 6:30pm, Sun 9 & 10:30am | Tip For modern church style,
see the monumental 2,000-seat Mary Queen of the Universe basilica, built for tourists and
consecrated in 1993 (8300 Vineland Avenue, www.maryqueenoftheuniverse.org).

63 __Muse of Discovery

Inspiration in an upturned hand

Designed to look like a gigantic woman nestled under a lush blanket of grass, Lake Eola Park's limestone and earthwork *Muse of Discovery* brings to mind the Greek goddesses of art, music, poetry, song, astronomy and astrology, history, theatrical tragedy and comedy, and dance. Their role was to whisper quiet words of inspiration into the ears of those who sought their counsel. Dried up artistically or suffering from writer's block? Consult the appropriate muses. Have everything you could possibly want but still feel unhappy? There's a muse for that, too. Want to discover your passion and potential? That's where Orlando's *Muse of Discovery* comes in.

Created by self-taught sculptor Meg White of Stephensport, Kentucky, the outdoor artwork located near the rainbow-colored Walt Disney Amphitheater honors the relationship between artists and knowledge-seekers and their muses, bringing them together through cooperative interaction – here you play a role by sitting in her hand. She is similar in size to her sister sculpture *Awakening Muse* at the Prairie Center for the Arts in Schaumburg, Illinois, which measures 40 feet long, 20 feet wide, and six feet tall at her highest point.

All we can see of Orlando's nature-based nurturer are parts of her bare legs, her head and left arm resting on a limestone pillow, and her right arm and hand. Having awakened from her slumber in the grassy mound, *Muse of Discovery*'s right palm is turned upward, inviting those in need of inspiration to nestle into her grasp and wait for her whispered revelations. Climb up, snap a quick photo if the mood strikes you, then listen for the end result of the fabled Greek muses' role in creativity: profound inspiration that gives birth to great works of art. Or simply view her from a distance and take inspiration from whatever revelations and emotions her contemplative gaze evokes.

Address 512 E Washington Street, Orlando, FL 32801, +1 (407) 246-4484, www.orlando.gov/Our-Government/Departments-Offices/Venues/See-Art-Orlando | Getting there Bus 51, 125 to E Robinson Street & N Rosalind Avenue | Tip Go from stressed to Zen with a hike at Split Oak Forest, named for its 200-year-old oak tree that's still living in spite of having been split in half (12901 Moss Park Road, www.orangecountyfl.net/CultureParks/Parks.aspx).

64 National Votes for Women Trail

Paving the path to the 19th Amendment

Women in Orlando and its neighboring town of Winter Park won the right to vote a year before the nation's 19th Amendment was signed into law, thanks to Unitarian minister and suffragist Reverend Mary Augusta Safford (1851–1927). During National Women's History Month in 2023, appropriately, two historical markers were unveiled to commemorate her efforts.

At the age of 60, Reverend Safford became president of the Equal Suffrage Association of Iowa in 1911, later becoming the first to hold that position for both the Orlando and the Florida branch of the Equal Suffrage League, as well as other high-profile roles. On four separate occasions, starting in 1913, she lobbied for women's suffrage in the Florida Legislature and then moved on to lobbying the US Congress and speaking for the cause at national and international events.

Dedicated on March 19, 2023, a marker at the First Unitarian Church of Orlando, which Safford helped to establish in its original Unity Chapel location at Central and Rosalind Avenues in 1913, remembers her efforts toward women's equality. A second National Votes for Women Trail marker, dedicated on March 7, 2023, at downtown Orlando's former Historic Angebilt Hotel (37 N Orange Avenue) recalls a November, 1913 Florida Federation of Women's Clubs meeting at what was then the Rosalind Club, a private social organization for well-heeled ladies. The meeting, during which Reverend Safford acted as chairperson, sparked the formation of the Florida Equal Suffrage Association.

These markers and 248 more nationwide form the National Votes for Women Trail, sponsored by the National Collaborative for Women's History Sites, while also commemorating the diverse groups and individuals instrumental in the suffragist fight for voting justice.

Address 1901 E Robinson Street, Orlando, FL 32803, www.ncwhs.org/votes-for-women-trail | Getting there Bus 51 to E Robinson Street & N Hampton Avenue. The marker is on the Hampton Avenue side of the church. | Hours Unrestricted | Tip Maxey Community Center honors Juanita Maxey, a tireless advocate for Black education and the first Black woman to vote after the 1920 Ocoee Massacre (830 Klondike Avenue, Winter Garden).

65 Nikki's Place

Parramore's first family of soul (food)

Family businesses don't come more heart-warming – and palate-pleasing – than Parramore's signature soul food restaurant, which has been a fixture since 1999. It actually dates back much further, thanks to head chef Nick Aiken, Jr., who got his start in the food-serving trade in the historically Black district in 1952.

Originally Roser's Restaurant, owned by Aiken's aunt Roser Mae Jones, it was here that he discovered his passion for cooking, learning his aunt's recipes by heart. It translated to a lifetime in the business, including greeting guests at the entrance to legendary Ronnie's Restaurant, when Black people weren't allowed to dine there, and working at Orlando's top sports venues, where he served Muhammad Ali and Elvis Presley. Aiken and wife Elaine bought Roser's in 1999 and renamed it after their daughter Shannea "Nikki" Aikins, who is now the manager. The family trio have kept it going despite a major fire in 2015 and the COVID-19 pandemic, when they transitioned to Parramore's top takeout service.

Regulars know Nikki's for its down-home qualities, where the likes of hog maws, ox tails, turkey necks, and chitterlings jostle with other classic Southern dishes, such as fried chicken and black-eyed peas. Liver and onions, pig feet, and smothered rib tips are also crowd pleasers, plus "the trinity" of collard greens, candied yams, and mac-and-cheese. You're also coming here for the friendly atmosphere and community ethic, which sees the restaurant regularly doing food events for the homeless. They have even catered for visiting celebrities, including Gladys Knight and Coretta Scott King.

Aiken already tried to retire once in 2007, but he found himself back in the kitchen, working eight-hour days and serving up his specialty crispy catfish. Nikki insists, "He just lives to cook. He'll probably keep doing it until he just can't do it anymore."

NIKKI'S PLACE RESTAURANT

SOUTHERN CUISINE
THE WAY IT USED TO BE
Since 1999

Address 742 Carter Street, Orlando, FL 32805, +1 (407) 425-5301, www.nikkisplace.net |
Getting there Bus 19 to S Parramore Avenue & Conley Street. Walk one block north to
Carter Street. | Hours Mon, Wed–Fri 8:30am–7pm, Sat & Sun 8:30am–6pm | Tip In the
evening, you'll enjoy the craft beers and live music of Parramore's Broken Strings Brewery,
with its signature murals (1012 W Church Street, www.brokenstringsbrewery.com).

66 Nona Adventure Park

Putting the "Wow!" in aqua fun

It labels itself "the ultimate outdoor adventure park," and, while Orlando has a few theme parks that might beg to differ, this off-beat Lake Nona attraction has created a genuine water-themed playground in an eye-catching lake setting. It is all part of the imaginative package of community features that have been poured into this master-planned neighborhood, especially Lake Nona South and its Laureate Park residential development.

The Nona Adventure Park might be tucked away – almost hidden behind Laureate Park Elementary School – but there's no mistaking its all-action profile once you find it. With four main elements plus Splashes Bar & Grill, voted the #2 French Fries in Orlando, this park is designed for active children and adults who want to get wet. It all starts with the 1,000-foot aqua park, an extensive array of floating inflatables that can be variously jumped on, climbed over, or leapt from in a multitude of ways. Then there's a high-quality cable wakeboarding course, featuring a state-of-the-art cable system that appeals to beginners and champion boarders alike. It's ideal for anyone looking to learn this growing sport or take their skills to the next level.

On dry land, there's the imposing Climbing Tower, a highly complex mix of a ropes course, with 36 floating platforms reaching a height of 60 feet, and three 50-foot climbing walls. Visit on the right day, and you might see some of the American Ninja Warriors training here. There is also a junior course for children ages three to eight.

The final piece of this outdoor adventure extravaganza is the Sunset Pavilion, a perfect setting for private events that include children's birthday parties by the dozen. Parents can give the kids relatively free rein, knowing there are plenty of lifeguards on hand to ensure safety, while the long, sandy beach offers a spot where moms and dads can chill.

Address 14086 Centerline Drive, Orlando, FL 32827, +1 (407) 313-2907, www.nonaadventurepark.com | Getting there By car, take the Central Florida GreeneWay to exit 19 and turn south onto Lake Nona Boulevard. Turn left onto Tavistock Lakes Boulevard, right onto Hitchings Avenue, left on Laureate Boulevard, right onto Kellogg Avenue, and left onto Centerline Drive. | Hours See website | Tip More watersports, including water-skiing and wakeboarding, are on offer at Orlando Watersports Complex, where they offer a "Get Up Guarantee" for beginners (8615 Florida Rock Road, www.orlandowatersports.com).

67 Ocoee Massacre
America's blood-stained election

A single plaque, titled *Ocoee Massacre and Exodus*, is a stark memorial to the bloodiest day in US election history. It recalls how a white supremacist mob attacked, murdered, and drove out Black residents of the town of Ocoee, 11 miles west of Orlando, in November, 1920. These events were largely suppressed until recent times, shamefully covered up by public officials and newspaper reports that referred to a "race riot," not the racially motivated massacre it was.

The lead-up to the presidential election had been marked by Ku Klux Klan marches to deter Black citizens from voting. But local farmer Mose Norman defied them, turning up at the polling station to demand his right to vote. Twice beaten and turned away, Norman fled to the home of civil rights advocate Julius "July" Perry, only for a white mob to storm the house in a blaze of gunfire. Norman had already escaped, but Perry was wounded, arrested, and jailed in Orlando. Following up on their handiwork, the mob besieged the jail, dragged Perry out, and lynched him. They then returned to Ocoee's Black quarter to cause deadly havoc.

They set fire to many homes, plus a school and church. Those who tried to escape the flames were shot; those who stayed burned to death. Another 500 Black residents fled for their lives, some carrying their children through alligator-infested swamps. The few who returned were forced to sell their property for pennies on the dollar. An official death toll was never taken, but some accounts list as many as 60 dead, and no Black residents were recorded again until 1978.

It wasn't until 2018 that a public proclamation recognized the massacre. In 2019, it was commemorated with a plaque in Bill Breeze Park, Ocoee, and there is a commemoration to Perry's lynching in Heritage Square Park. The massacre is arguably the most horrifying act of violence in US election history.

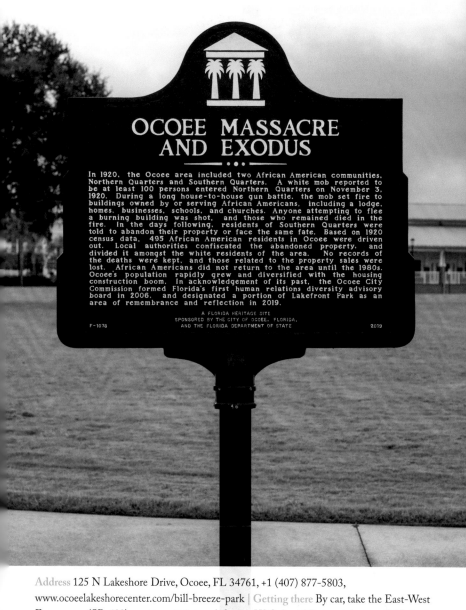

OCOEE MASSACRE AND EXODUS

In 1920, the Ocoee area included two African American communities, Northern Quarters and Southern Quarters. A white mob reported to be at least 100 persons entered Northern Quarters on November 3, 1920. During a long house-to-house gun battle, the mob set fire to buildings owned by or serving African Americans, including a lodge, homes, businesses, schools, and churches. Anyone attempting to flee a burning building was shot, and those who remained died in the fire. In the days following, residents of Southern Quarters were told to abandon their property or face the same fate. Based on 1920 census data, 495 African American residents in Ocoee were driven out. Local authorities confiscated the abandoned property, and divided it amongst the white residents of the area. No records of the deaths were kept, and those related to the property sales were lost. African Americans did not return to the area until the 1980s. Ocoee's population rapidly grew and diversified with the housing construction boom. In acknowledgement of its past, the Ocoee City Commission formed Florida's first human relations diversity advisory board in 2006, and designated a portion of Lakefront Park as an area of remembrance and reflection in 2019.

A FLORIDA HERITAGE SITE
SPONSORED BY THE CITY OF OCOEE, FLORIDA,
AND THE FLORIDA DEPARTMENT OF STATE

F-1078   2019

Address 125 N Lakeshore Drive, Ocoee, FL 34761, +1 (407) 877-5803, www.ocoeelakeshorecenter.com/bill-breeze-park | Getting there By car, take the East-West Expressway (SR-408) west to exit 1, turn left onto W Colonial Drive, right onto S Bluford Avenue, right onto McKey Street, then left on N Lakeshore Drive | Hours Unrestricted | Tip The Orange County History Center in downtown Orlando has more information about the Ocoee massacre in the African American History section (65 E Central Boulevard, www.thehistorycenter.org).

68 _Old Joe_ Statue
Mount Dora's angriest alligator

Seeing alligators in the wild is a very Floridian experience, but being able to sit on the back of a 15-footer without losing life or limbs is a rare treat indeed.

Mount Dora's _Old Joe_ alligator, cast in bronze and situated just off the eastern bank of Lake Dora on the Palm Island Park boardwalk, is based on a real alligator. Legend has it that as the late 1800s slipped into a new century, the living version of this goliath of a reptile sealed his reputation as a fierce predator, worthy of his genus' more than 50 million years of evolution, by terrorizing the town with his indiscriminate appetite for small animals, large livestock, and deer. Old Joe wasn't Lake Dora's only alligator to take part in mammal munching activities, but he had a hard-earned reputation for being the meanest of the bunch.

The sculpture was created by the American Bronze Foundry in Sanford, Florida, using a three-millennium-old process called "lost wax casting." It was originally intended to be placed near Mount Dora's lighthouse. And if the draw of sitting on a massive alligator's back was enough to entice children away from the water's murky edge where live gators resided, so much the better. But plans changed, and Old Joe – or at least his 1,200-pound likeness – now basks further inland on a concrete pad across from Gilbert Park, soaking up whatever rays of sunlight are able to penetrate the copse of trees that surround him. His menacing mouth is open to reveal rows of prey-crunching teeth, while the plaque near his tail reminds visitors to _leave the real ones alone_.

Thanks to Mount Dora's resident philanthropists Richard MacSherry and Loyd "Mike" Kiernan, who donated the $52,000 required to make the statue, this legacy to the locally loved crocodilian lives on. Keep an eye out when visiting Old Joe, though; his smaller cousins and distant progeny still live in Lake Dora.

Address S Tremain Street, Mount Dora, FL 32757 | **Getting there** By car, take US-441 north to SR-46 (E 1st Avenue). Turn left onto E 1st Avenue, left onto S Highland Street, then right onto Liberty Avenue. "Old Joe" is near the corner of E Liberty Avenue and S Tremain Street. | **Hours** Unrestricted | **Tip** American Bronze Foundry also cast the dynamic *Victory Knight* statue located outside the Alumni Center at the University of Central Florida (12676 Gemini Boulevard N, www.ucfalumni.com/alumnicenter).

69 Orlando Museum of Art
The secret language of animal art

Discover the "hidden code" inherent in animal-inspired urns, figurines, and vessels in the Orlando Museum of Art's "Art of the Ancient Americas" collection. These pieces indicated important social markers, such as rank, cultural, and spiritual beliefs in the North, Central, and South American indigenous cultures.

It all starts with the jaguar, the undisputed symbol of power and position within a community. This graceful predator is depicted through a headdress on a Mayan warrior (600-1000), an urn that was possibly used during a royal burial (1100-1400), a "portrait" vessel depicting the image of a high-ranking ruler, and an amusing but no less fierce tripod urn (1100-1400). Its cousin the puma exudes strength, too, through a rounded vessel that looks like an adorable house cat but communicated a much different story to those who first saw it. Its owner likely held a very high position indeed.

One of the collection's most striking depictions of an animal is the ceramic *Bat Vessel* (500 BCE–100 CE), with its wings extended and teeth bared. While the bat was revered in ancient societies, it was also considered a symbol of the warrior and of blood sacrifice. The museum's bat vessel comes from Peru's Moche civilization, who honored and admired the winged mammals' ability to see at night and therefore hunt under cover of darkness. With those attributes in mind, this vessel would have been used as an offering for an important individual.

A small alligator, or *caiman* in Spanish, carved out of volcanic rock (600-1400) looks almost as ancient as its real-life ancestors. Caimans would have been viewed as sea monsters when this one was made, and the hidden language the predator communicated was that of fear and power. Look for other unusual but meaningful pieces, such as a spider cast in gold and a fascinating, stylized human crab.

Address 2416 N Mills Avenue, Orlando, FL 32803, +1 (407) 896-4231, www.omart.org, info@omart.org | **Getting there** Bus 125 to Princeton Street & N Mills Avenue | **Hours** Tue–Fri 10am–4pm, Sat & Sun noon–4pm | **Tip** Get your hands dirty while beautifying Orlando neighborhoods with the GreenUp Orlando volunteer tree-planting program (various locations, www.orlando.gov/Parks-the-Environment/GreenUp-Orlando).

70 Orlando Station
The railroad's Mission Revival statement

Tourism isn't a recent phenomenon for Florida. In fact, the Sunshine State was practically founded on it. Railroad barons Henry Flagler (1830–1913) and Henry Plant (1819–1899) both created railways aimed at bringing rich Northerners to Florida in the late 19th and early 20th centuries, while Tampa created the Tin Can Tourist camping organization in 1919. Not to be left out during the 1920s land boom, Orlando's leadership decided it needed to appeal to all those potential tourists and investors, and Atlantic Coastline Railroad architect Alpheus Marston "A. M." Griffin (1885–1954) was commissioned to create a fancy new station.

Given free rein to come up with something impressive, Griffin set off for the West Coast to gather inspiration and returned enthused by the Spanish architecture of Southern California. Griffin's station, which cost a whopping $500,000 – more than $8 million in modern terms – was unveiled as a model of Mission Revival construction in January, 1927, featuring striking twin domed bell towers, arches, a parapet, and a tiled roof. The unique gateway soon attracted thousands of visitors and speculators, putting The City Beautiful on the map like never before. In 1920, Orlando's population numbered barely 9,200, and it soared to 27,330 by 1930. The Great Depression didn't dampen the flow.

The Atlantic Coastline Railroad merged with rival Seaboard in 1967, creating the Seaboard Coastline as rail passenger traffic to Florida dwindled. Savvy management and another merger in the 1980s kept the system alive and the Orlando Station in one piece, while many others were demolished. The only station of its kind in the state, it was designated as an Orlando Historic Landmark in 1978. It is a tragic postscript that the 2016 plaque commemorating A. M. Griffin's grand structure contains a howling error, referring to the famed architect as *M. A. Griffith*.

Address 1400 Sligh Boulevard, Orlando, FL 32806, +1 (800) 872-7254 | Getting there SunRail to Orlando; bus 40 to Sligh Boulevard & W Copeland Drive | Hours Daily 10am–8pm | Tip Among Orlando's most distinctive homes, the 1925 S. J. Sligh house is an example of Neoclassical Revival in nearby Lake Copeland Historic District (239 E Copeland Drive).

71 Orlando Sun Resort

Kissimmee's abandoned vacation destination

In its heyday, the sprawling Orlando Sun Resort and Convention Center on the tourist-centric Irlo Bronson Memorial Highway (US-192) was a modern marvel. Today, a derelict shell of its former self, fenced in and falling into ruin, is all that occupies this once-prime real estate.

The complex began its life in 1972 as the prestigious 77-acre Orlando Hyatt House, which rose from the phase one construction of the never-opened Carolando Motor Inn, not long after Disney's Magic Kingdom theme park first flung its gates open. It gained popularity as one of Orlando's best-placed hotels, situated just off the main route of Interstate 4 leading to Walt Disney World. Boasting eight sections, each featuring five buildings placed around central courtyards, it offered a whopping 960 rooms and a massive central building with a lobby, shopping, dining, and convention space. With its exceptional location, it couldn't fail.

Rebranded as Hyatt Orlando in 1977, its success continued. However, like hotels nationwide, the vacation destination felt the shockwave of the September 11, 2001 terrorist attacks in New York and Washington, DC. These events had a particularly catastrophic effect on the country's tourism industry. The resort once again fell on hard times.

It was rescued from bankruptcy in 2004 by The Moinian Group, a prodigious real estate company that had big plans for their freshly acquired tourist playground. Instead, the newly named Orlando Sun Resort underwent eight years of spiraling mismanagement, neglect, and bad publicity. It had a short stint as the Ramada Orlando Celebration Resort until it was finally abandoned in 2012.

It is illegal to enter the property, which is fenced to keep out trespassers, so view the complex only from the road. But from photos online, you can see the interior looks as if a catastrophic hurricane swept through the day it closed.

Address 6375 W Irlo Bronson Memorial Highway, Kissimmee, FL 34747 | Getting there Bus 55, 56 to W Irlo Bronson Memorial Highway & Parkway Boulevard | Hours Unrestricted from the outside only | Tip Once a tourist draw, A World of Orchids nursery died a slow death due to Hurricane Charley in 2004, closing as a sad remnant of its former self in 2012. You can see the sad sight by pulling off the road and peering inside (2501 N Old Lake Wilson Road, Kissimmee).

72 Out of the Closet
The thrift store with a purpose

Pick up an incredible bargain in vintage clothing, furniture, and housewares, or donate your own gently used goods while doing good for the community at Out of the Closet thrift store. Sales here benefit the AIDS Healthcare Foundation (AHF) for the prevention and treatment of HIV and AIDS. Opened in February, 2021, this Orlando shop joins 22 other Out of the Closet locations across the country. The first store opened in the Atwater Village area of Los Angeles in 1990.

You're here to hunt for fabulous and affordable treasures, and part of the fun is not knowing what you might find from week to week. It's certainly about vintage and modern attire, and that's not all. Need a sofa or a wingback chair? Guitars, artwork, kitchen gadgets? You might just find them here. And you'll certainly see pots and pans, which bring to mind Out of the Closet's original mascot, Potsy Pansy.

Moving? Spring cleaning? Tired of all those jeans and T-shirts you haven't worn since high school? When it's time for your goods to come out of your closet, this thrift shop is ready to give them a second life. They'll even arrange pickup of large items. For every dollar Out of the Closet stores take in, a whopping 96 percent of it goes towards HIV services in the US and abroad. That's what heartfelt community involvement can achieve.

In 1996, the HIV epidemic peaked, and infection rates began to fall, thanks in large part to powerful education campaigns and advances in treatment. By 2021, approximately 95 percent of people experiencing HIV infection and having regular access to antiretroviral treatment were virally suppressed. But the statistics are still concerning. In 2023, Florida ranked third in HIV infections nationwide, and that's where testing and treatment centers such as Out of the Closet come in: the shop has an AHF pharmacy and offers free rapid-result HIV testing.

Address 1349 N Mills Avenue, Orlando, FL 32803, +1 (407) 583-4916,
www.outofthecloset.org | Getting there Bus 125 to N Mills Avenue & Virginia Drive |
Hours Mon–Sat 10am–7pm, Sun 10am–6pm | Tip The Center takes donations of non-
perishable food, pet supplies, and cleaning items for The Pride Pantry, serving LGBTQ+
community members (942 N Mills Avenue, www.thecenterorlando.org).

73 Oviedo Ghost Lights

Freakish phenomenon or simple science?

As if the tannin-stained Econlockhatchee River isn't spooky enough, there's a garish, green glow emanating from underneath Snow Hill Road Bridge in Oviedo after nightfall that turns the languid waterway into a spectacle of supernatural proportions.

In Medieval times, swamp lights that deceived wanderers in the dark of night were called "will-o'-the-wisps." In Britain during the 1600s, the lights were sometimes known as "jack-o'-lanterns," referring not to various Irish legends of Stingy Jack or to the carved pumpkin we know today, but to night-watchmen – sometimes also referred to generically as "Jack" – who carried lanterns and were therefore known as "Jack of the Lantern." Today, the glowing globes are often called "ghost lights." Scientists, however, use another name: chemiluminescence, which refers to light that is the result of a chemical reaction.

Mostly mischievous, sometimes menacing, freakish orbs of "otherworldly" origin aren't unique to Florida, having been reported across North and South America, Europe, and Asia. But all of them have something in common: they scare the living daylights out of those who see them, either accidentally or on a dare, and they prefer to make their home around murky ground, such as swamps, bogs, mud flats, and marshy areas.

The Oviedo ghost lights have long been a source of speculation. Some say the eerie phosphorescence is the result of swamp gas caused by the collision of oxygen with highly combustible methane, phosphines, and other chemical compounds in decaying plants. Others insist the green glow has chased them up the riverbank and instilled a life-long fear of the dark. Wherever the truth lies, adventure seekers should watch for them on Florida's warmest nights, when they're most active. But don't fool yourself into thinking you're safe, even in times of the year when the temperature goes down.

Address Snow Hill Road and Bob White Trail, Chuluota, FL 32766 | Getting there By car, take FL-417 to exit 41 and stay right for Red Bug Lake Road, which becomes W Mitchell Hammock Road. Turn left onto Lockwood Boulevard, right onto County Road 419, and left onto Snow Hill Road. Pass Bob White Trail and proceed to the unpaved turnoff just before the bridge, then walk down to the river. | Hours Unrestricted | Tip Hike the Econ River Wilderness trail to see swamp gas bubbles on the river's surface in daylight (3795 Old Lockwood Road, Oviedo, www.seminolecountyfl.gov/locations/Econ-River-Wilderness-Area.stml).

74 The Paddling Center
Natural Florida at its finest

Everglades National Park may be 216 miles to the South, but the headwaters of that vast World Heritage Site are located in Kissimmee. Save yourself the eight-hour round-trip drive and take in the flora and fauna of Shingle Creek on a self-guided kayak or paddleboard excursion. Or spend a couple of hours exploring the river's cypress forest by day or "after hours" on a guided kayak eco tour from The Paddling Center, with reptiles, raptors, and, if you're lucky, otters or deer as your companions.

In 2014, John Jacobs submitted a proposal to create The Paddling Center, won the concession, purchased kayaks and accoutrement necessary for success, and opened his new venture that same summer. Running the business was a steep learning curve for the avid kayaker, but with safety and fantastic customer experiences as his guiding lights, the business began to thrive. Two years later the center began offering eco tours.

The center sits mid-way on a five-mile stretch of Shingle Creek, named by 1800s settlers who used cypress for their house's roof shingles and logged the trees down the creek. The location offers unique views for paddlers making an out-and-back journey of 1.25 miles upriver or 1.25 miles downriver. The two-hour kayak eco-tour explores a cypress forest, which feels almost prehistoric. Also look for the remnants of the 1890s Florida Midland Railroad. The Paddling Center's staff will show kayak newbies the basics, and by the time you're settled in and paddling toward your first wildlife sighting, your worries will have melted away.

If you're wondering if you can actually paddle all the way to the Florida Everglades from its headwaters at Shingle Creek, the answer is yes, if you have your own kayak, plenty of time and stamina, and you're prepared to cross five lakes including the massive Lake Okeechobee, traverse rivers and drainage canals, and do a bit of portaging.

Address 4266 W Vine Street, Kissimmee, FL 34741, +1 (407) 343-7740, www.paddlingcenter.com | Getting there Bus 55, 56 to W Vine & Interior Streets | Hours Daily 9am–5pm, last rental 2:30pm | Tip See more of Shingle Creek's waters with a Spirit of the Swamp airboat tour on Lake Tohopekaliga (2830 Neptune Road, Kissimmee, www.spiritoftheswamp.com).

75 *Parenthood* Scenes
Orlando's movie-making magic

Popular movies such as *Jurassic Park III*, *Minority Report*, *2 Fast 2 Furious*, and *Van Helsing* include scenes that were filmed in the soundstages located at Universal Studios Florida. But some, including the star-studded *Parenthood* (1989), shot key scenes in Central Florida. In the movie, Steve Martin and Mary Steenburgen as Gil and Karen Buckman, along with Gil's two siblings, are trying to survive the hair-raising roller coaster ride that is the hallmark of their dysfunctional families.

The University of Florida campus in Gainesville also made the *Parenthood* cut, but as far as Florida fame is concerned, Orlando was the winner, with 16 filming locations scattered around town. Tinker Field, now Tinker Field History Plaza at the east end of Camping World Stadium, was the site of the movie's opening scene, which was meant to represent the Buckman family's arrival at a Cardinals baseball game in their hometown of St. Louis, Missouri. It immediately establishes Gil and Karen's chaotic life with children as they unload the kids and armfuls of paraphernalia from the car then load them back up after the game before driving down a major highway toward home (in reality, a cameo by Orlando's Interstate 4). While you're at Tinker Field History Plaza, look for plaques honoring famous baseball players and prominent civil rights activists.

Houses in College Park and Winter Park stood in for some of the character's homes, including exterior shots of Gil's sister Helen's house, portrayed by a white bungalow on the corner of Easton Avenue and Greely Street. Orlando Mayor William Beardall Senior Center (800 Delaney Avenue) posed as the exterior of Gil and Karen's son Kevin's elementary school; the auditorium at Howard Middle School (800 E Robinson Street) played a brief role; and a public sports field in Delaney Park saw some of Kevin's Little League baseball action.

Address Tinker Field, 287 S Tampa Avenue, Orlando, FL 32805 | Getting there By car, take the East-West Expressway (SR-408) to exit 9. Turn left onto Long Street, then right onto S Tampa Avenue. | Hours Unrestricted | Tip The demolition of Orlando's former City Hall provided footage for the explosion of International Controls Systems, Inc. in *Lethal Weapon 3*. The new City Hall now sits next door (400 S Orange Avenue).

76_Pioneer Village

Real 19th-century Florida know-how

If you ever thought it was impossible to survive in Florida without air-conditioning, just visit the Pioneer Village at Shingle Creek in Kissimmee to learn how intrepid, 19th-century settlers here not only survived but thrived through the clever use of down-home techniques and know-how.

Pioneer Village itself is a living history museum, a clever collection of buildings and paraphernalia from the late 1800s, all brought from around Osceola County and reassembled in a realistic depiction of pioneer life. Look for the general store, schoolhouse, church, train depot, settler homesteads, Seminole settlement, working blacksmith shop, and citrus packing plant. The park is also part of the 7.8-acre Mary Kendall Steffee Nature Preserve, where many of the trees and shrubs provided essential dyes, clothing, and medicine for the early settlers.

Pay special attention to the Lanier Cracker House. This original, 1889 home of the cattle-ranching Lanier family is a classic example of how these hardy folk constructed dwellings that survived the state's extreme climate. Built in dog-trot style – a central passageway between the two halves of the four-room house – this configuration helped catch the breeze and take advantage of natural air-conditioning. The house was also raised off the ground for additional cooling and to avoid the flood-prone nature of the area. To stand up to the weather and the army of bugs ready to chew their way through soft woods, the family used strong, rough-hewn cypress for the siding and yellow pine for the floors. In its entirety, the home is a rare surviving example of frameless box construction, which would have been standard for the late 19th century.

Enjoy more demonstrations of how people lived off the land before electricity during Pioneer Day each November, an annual celebration of Seminole and pioneer life at the Village.

Address 2491 Babb Road, Kissimmee, FL 34746, +1 (407) 570-6255,
www.osceolahistory.org/pioneer-village | Getting there By car, from I-4 W, take exit 68 for
SR-535 and turn left. Go south to W Irlo Bronson Memorial Highway (192) and turn left.
Turn left onto Storey Lake Road, then right at the traffic circle onto Nature's Ridge Drive,
which becomes Babb Road. | Hours Daily 10am–4pm | Tip Also pay a visit to Shingle
Creek Regional Park's 1911 Steffee Homestead and its caretaker cabin (4280 W Vine Street,
www.paddlingcenter.com/shingle-creek-regional-park).

77 — Plant Street Market

The brewery that sparked a foodie phenom

To say things snowballed after a skiing vacation would be a cliché if it wasn't the story of three buddies on a trip to Colorado that led to the creation of Winter Garden's foodie-centric Plant Street Market and Crooked Can Brewery, affectionately known as "The Can."

Killing time before a flight back to Orlando in 2014, Andy Sheeter, Robert Scott, and Jared Czachorowski were enjoying the laid-back buzz of a craft brewery in Breckenridge when it struck Sheeter they were witnessing a fab formula sadly lacking in their part of Florida. He set about creating a business plan on the plane home. Within weeks, the threesome were pitching their idea to the city and found an enthusiastic audience. Two months later, they had a property under contract at the run-down site of the aptly named Shady Hill Apartments. And things took another unexpected turn. The site was long and narrow, not ideal for just a brewery. But if they expanded, it was perfect for a brewery and a market, and the two parts would support each other.

Plant Street Market opened in May 2015, a mix of craft stores and food stalls in addition to the headline attraction of The Can. Their investment totaled $4 million. The city weighed in with $86,000 of street improvements, including new sidewalks, streetlights, and utilities, and building grants added another $100,000. The 1920s-style, brick structure, in keeping with the city's period main street with shaded outdoor seating, was attention grabbing in every way.

Now, alongside the award-winning brews from The Can, which are highlighted by their iconic high-stepping, bowler-hatted mascot McSwagger, visitors can enjoy a community-centered array of fresh produce and dining delights, including ceviche, empanadas, sushi, pizza, gourmet popcorn, and popsicles, as well as a butcher's and coffee roastery. It's quite an achievement for one skiing adventure.

Address 426 W Plant Street, Winter Garden, FL 34787, +1 (407) 395-9520, www.crookedcan.com/plant-st-market | Getting there By car, take the East-West Expressway (SR-408) west to the Florida Turnpike and take the Turnpike north to exit 267B. Follow signs for SR-50 west, turn right onto S Park Avenue and right onto Plant Street. | Hours Mon–Thu 10am–7pm, Fri & Sat 10am–6pm, Sun 11am–6pm; brewery Sun–Thu 11am–11pm, Fri & Sat 11am–midnight | Tip Plant Street Market is located on the 23-mile West Orange Trail. Rent a bike from Wheelworks to explore this scenic gem (455 E Plant Street, Winter Garden, www.wgwheelworks.com).

78 Player 1 Video Game Bar

Beers. Games. Music.

If you really know your PS4 from your 3DO, you will be right at home at Player 1 Video Game Bar in Lake Buena Vista, near Walt Disney World. Established in 2013 by two arch gaming buddies and movie special effects guys Jeff Benoit and Rhett Bennett, the venue is a crazy, neon-tinted mash-up of craft beer bar and games arcade for the obvious title of "barcade," with the accent equally on quality craft brews and the likes of Atari, Super Smash Bros, and Mario Kart.

Player 1 is designed to be a fun destination for locals, tourists, and service industry workers alike to mingle over an alcoholic beverage and a game of Pac-Man. It was the families of the game-playing duo who invested in their entrepreneurial venture. Family members also pitched in to help fit out the space, which Jeff and Rhett filled with vintage games that they tracked down all over the country. The machines are updated regularly, and there are always some 35 to 40 cabinet games on offer, including the latest consoles that are available for enthusiastic customers.

Staff members keep the atmosphere suitably nerdy with their own takes on cosplay, and visitors are definitely welcome to dress up in keeping with the various games and pop culture characters. There are also themed weekly events, such as Weeb Wednesday dedicated to all things anime, and Bingo Oni-Chan, a geeky version of bingo played for laughs. Tournaments and game-release parties are also highlights, along with themed special events, like Emo Valentine's Day.

But the real gem at the heart of this barcade is actually the bar. Or rather, the amazing, glass-encased, historic tribute to the full array of arcade games – from Bagatelle and Baffle Ball in the 1930s to the latest console blockbusters – that runs the full length of the 33-foot-long bar, underlining Player 1's essential ethos: Beer. Games. Music.

Address 8652 Palm Parkway, Orlando, FL 32836, +1 (407) 504-7521, www.player1orlando.com | Getting there Bus 350 to Palm Parkway & S Apopka Vineland Road | Hours Daily 1pm–2am | Tip If you're feeling snacky at 2am after Player 1 closes, the world's largest White Castle is just 1.5 miles to the north and is open 24 hours (11595 Daryl Carter Parkway, www.whitecastle.com).

79 The Poozeum

Fossilized feces make learning fun

Children (and some adults) find poop hilarious, but "Barnum," an enormous coprolite (dinosaur dropping) deposited by some long-gone Tyrannosaurus rex is no joke. In fact, it's so gigantic it earned the Guinness World Record title of the "Largest Coprolite by a Carnivorous Animal." It was honored with a certificate stating its status, which now sits proudly above the prehistoric specimen in the Orlando Science Center's fascinating Poozeum.

The Poozeum, a dedicated area just outside the DinoDigs permanent exhibit on the museum's fourth floor, includes a collection of other coprolites, too, offering a scientific look at the bodily waste of crocodilians, frogs, fish, small mammals, a shark or lungfish, and other unidentified species. Predictably, it's all a source of fascination for kids, who absolutely adore the idea of fossilized excrement, especially when dinosaurs are involved. The Poozeum's oldest coprolite dates back 200 million years, and its youngest is just 11,700.

Education becomes enjoyable through four panels that break down the steps archeologists go through when identifying coprolites: chemical composition, inclusions (such as undigested bits of gnawed-up animal bones and other matter), shape, and the location in which the fossil was found. Two more panels describe Barnum (which is more than two feet long, and just over six inches wide) and the characteristics that led to its classification as a coprolite rather than a rock.

Barnum is owned by George Frandsen, who also achieved a Guinness World Record in 2015 for owning the largest collection of coprolites with his 1,277 examples. It's Frandsen who founded the scatological section, which, appropriately, is located near the museum's fourth-floor restrooms. Visitors can also see the skeletons of land and sea monsters in DinoDigs, along with the Science Center's eight other interactive exhibits.

Address 777 E Princeton Street, Orlando, FL 32803, +1 (407) 514-2000, www.osc.org | Getting there SunRail to AdventHealth; bus 125 to Princeton Street & Camden Road | Hours Mon & Tue 10am–5pm, Thu–Sun 10am–5pm | Tip The Orlando Science Center helped restore what is now the Randall R. Tuten Orlando Fire Museum. It features a rare 1926 American LaFrance fire engine (814 E Rollins Street, www.orlandofiremuseum.org).

80_Presidents Hall of Fame

A model America

You'd normally have to visit Washington, DC to see the White House or go to South Dakota for Mount Rushmore, but a roadside attraction in the city of Clermont offers a unique alternative, along with an exclusive take on all things presidential. Not only does it boast both icons in one eye-catching location, but the Presidents Hall of Fame also features an astonishing collection of models, wax figures, and memorabilia that pay homage to various Commanders in Chief.

A replica of Caroline Kennedy's boudoir during JFK's presidency? You got it. A full-size reproduction of the Resolute Desk? That's also here. Evening gowns of various First Ladies? Yes, those too, along with presidential china, a diorama of the Founding Fathers, and champagne glasses sipped from by President Reagan and Soviet leader Mikhail Gorbachev. Much of the collection was donated by past presidents.

A genuine labor of love that became a feted local exhibit and then slipped into near obscurity, the Hall of Fame remains doggedly alive in the shadow of the 226-foot-high landmark of the Citrus Tower. It was established in 1964 as House of Presidents wax museum and became the Hall of Fame under new owners John and Jan Zweifel in 1992 to exhibit their vast array of Americana, a compilation which included John's crowning glory: a 1:12-scale, 1,200-square-foot, 10-ton model of 1600 Pennsylvania Avenue.

Completed in 1976 after 10 years of meticulous research, Zweifel's astounding creation went on a 20-year tour of all 50 states, as well as overseas to Britain, the Netherlands, and Japan. President Reagan called it a "national treasure." It finally settled in its current home, where John and Jan regularly updated it with each new administration. Sadly, the couple passed in 2020, but their six children and curator Tommy Candido continue to maintain the Hall and its magnificent centerpiece.

Address 123 N Highway 27, Clermont, FL 34711, +1 (352) 394-2836, www.facebook.com/
ThePresidentsHallofFame | Getting there By car, take East-West Expressway (SR-408)
west from downtown to the Florida Turnpike and continue to exit 272. Take SR-50 west to
Highway 27 and go north for one mile to destination. | Hours Mon–Sat 10am–4pm, Sun
noon–4pm | Tip Dive into local pioneering heritage at nearby Clermont Historic Village
Museum (490 West Avenue, Clermont, www.clermonthistoricvillage.org).

81 Prometheus Esoterica
The beautiful art of the macabre

If an oddities shop and a Goth boutique had a baby, it would be Prometheus Esoterica. This wonderfully twisted brainchild of Whitney Hayes and her husband Adam DeLancett blends their love of the macabre with antiques, art, and "ethically sourced specimens" of the creepiest kind. From fantasy headgear to skeletal remains, this repository is either the stuff of dreams or fodder for nightmares. However it strikes you, "boring" will not be among your adjectives while browsing through a massive assemblage of items as varied as a Civil War amputation kit, dolls whose mere presence will keep you awake at night, a full-sized taxidermy lion, real human and animal skeletons, and a small bowl of adorable human finger and toe bones.

Whitney and Adam came up with the idea of opening a shop focused on the macabre when they were still dating, inspired by their forays into old country funeral homes, private collections, and estate and garage sales. As lovers of Halloween, history, cemeteries, and horror movies, their shop would be a welcoming place where collectors and the creepy-curious could find unique oddities and make them their own. Among their current inventory is an Ecuadorian shrunken head, the starting point for discussions about the history and culture behind the practice. Some items, such as the head, are not for sale, though in a bittersweet turn of events, the couple eventually sold a beloved, taxidermy ostrich that had been a display-only item to longtime customers, who had been saving for years. They were finally able to buy it right before their nuptials. It was a sad parting, but an uplifting story nonetheless.

They also do taxidermy, wet specimens, and pet memorials, having acquired the skills on roadkill through trial and error in their backyard processing operation. Many are on display in the shop. Drop in, enjoy a chat, and prepare to be amazed!

Address 3744 Howell Branch Road, Winter Park, FL 32792, +1 (407) 951-8883, www.prometheusesoterica.com, prometheusesoterica@gmail.com | Getting there By car, from I-4 E take exit 88, turn right onto Lee Road, left onto Orlando Avenue, and right onto E Horatio Avenue which becomes Howell Branch Road | Hours Wed & Thu 11am–6pm, Fri & Sat 11am–7pm, Sun noon–5pm | Tip Take a freaky, flavor-filled trip back to your parents' childhood with Rocket Fizz: Soda Pop & Candy Shop's throwback sweets and bottled sodas (250 S Park Avenue, Winter Park, www.rocketfizz.com).

82 Pulse Interim Memorial

Remembering the fallen 49

For all Orlando's dedication to inclusivity, its LGBTQIA+ community faced horrors and tragedy on June 12, 2016 at the Pulse Nightclub, when a hate-filled shooter murdered 49 people and injured 53 more. In their honor, an interim memorial was erected, and you can leave a message on the light-up panels below the Pulse sign there today. A permanent memorial is intended to be a place of education, reflection, and healing.

Pulse was the second deadliest mass shooting in the US to date, just behind the Las Vegas massacre in 2017. The outpouring of grief in Orlando was immense, and memorials sprang up throughout the downtown area, from the many murals painted on buildings to 49 rainbow-colored seats in INTER&Co Stadium, home of the Orlando City soccer club, where a moment of silence was observed during the 49th minute of the Lions' first soccer game after the shooting. As floral tributes laid at Pulse faded, they were taken to Harry P. Leu Gardens and composted to provide nutrients for other plants. Out of the tragedy came the motto, "Orlando Strong," still used to describe the city's resilience and support of diversity.

Plans are in the works for a permanent memorial, but the commemoration site remains a setting for deep empathy. People still leave tokens of love and compassion for the victims, survivors, first responders, and the medical staff at Orlando Regional Medical Center, Florida Hospital, Dr. Phillips Hospital, and Winter Park Hospital, whose mission it was to save the lives of the wounded.

On May 12, 2021, the US House of Representatives passed H.R.49, a bill that would designate Pulse as a national memorial. On June 9, 2021, it passed in the Senate, and, on the fifth anniversary of the shooting, President Joe Biden vowed to sign the bill. On June 25, 2021, he did just that. Survivors of the tragedy were in attendance as the bill became law.

Address 1912 S Orange Avenue, Orlando, FL 32806 | Getting there Bus 7, 11, 18, 40 to S Orange Avenue & E Kaley Street | Hours Daily 7:30am–midnight | Tip Four victims of the Pulse shooting are buried in Unit 6 of Greenwood Cemetery, near granite markers with the names of each of the 49 who were killed (1603 Greenwood Street, www.orlando.gov).

83 Rage Room Orlando
Let it all out!

Life can be hard. That's where Rage Room Orlando's Coping Lab comes in. Here you can take up a bat or a sledgehammer and smash the living daylights out of everything in sight, thus letting out all your pent-up stress. The added bonus is that your mom won't yell at you for making a mess, and you don't have to clean up when you're done.

The Coping Lab setting is minimalistic, from the small lobby where ragers check in for their appointment with a sledgehammer to the room where it all happens. It's nothing fancy, but you're here to work out every insult that's been slung your way, every time you've been cut off in traffic, that weird habit your significant other can't seem to drop, and the way your boss sometimes forgets you're an overworked human being, not a mindless automaton.

You supply the closed-toed shoes and comfy clothing, and Rage Room supplies coveralls and protective gear for your head, face, and hands. Then, you enter a room where a plywood wall covered in graffiti encourages you to "Let. It. Out!" Smash glass into a million pieces, splinter wooden chairs until they're toothpicks – whatever it takes to bring on the mellow.

Packages range from 10 minutes for those who are just a little bit ticked off or new to venting their spleen, to 40 minutes for full melt-down relief. You can choose from a range of breakables, including glassware, 32-inch television sets, and a full-sized car that up to 10 people can beat into submission. If you prefer to rage against your own electronics (and who hasn't dreamed of smashing a printer that jams?), there's a package for that, too. Even kids aged 5 to 13 can smash with their own Rugrat Rager package.

Ragers with a gentler disposition can opt for the Paint Throwing package, or maybe spend 30 minutes flinging paint at a canvas, the wall, and friends. You'll walk away with your work of art and a much happier outlook.

Address 4065 L. B. McLeod Road, Suite G, Orlando, FL 32811, +1 (407) 712-6394, www.rageroomorlando.org, amrageroomorlando@gmail.com | Getting there Bus 24, 303 to Bruton Boulevard & Prince Hall Boulevard | Hours Tue–Fri 2–9pm, Sat noon–9pm | Tip For the exact opposite style of stress-relief, book a "float" in a sensory deprivation pod at Float8 Orlando Wellness Spa in Baldwin Park (4832 New Broad Street, www.float8ion.com/baldwin-park).

84 Renninger's Antiques

Everything you never knew you needed

Gone are the days when adult children eagerly awaited the inheritance of their parents' prized antiques and collectables. Luckily, Renninger's Flea Market and Antique Center's semi-chaotic conglomeration of vendor booths and stand-alone shops feels more like trolling through a series of crazy aunts' attics and basements than hand-me-downs. There are traditional antique dealers selling massive China cabinets and four-poster beds to be sure, but it's the vast array of vintage oddities that really make this place a picker's paradise.

The 117-acre property offers a four-part experience, starting with the 700-booth, indoor Antique Center. Looking for second-hand chairs from a Walt Disney World hotel room? They're here. Need to replace your brass diving helmet, relive your childhood with a Dukes of Hazzard lunchbox, or start a new hobby collecting rhinestone jewelry? Drop by!

Outside, a Street of Shops adds a pleasant "village" feel to your antiquing, with a series of cute cottage-style buildings specializing in handicrafts and decorative accoutrement. The treasure trove then spills out onto ample lawn space, where patio furniture, antler art, full-sized horse statues, and a remarkable amount of random wooden items can be found, along with just about everything else you could imagine. This area gets even more informal, as some of the vendors here simply open the trunks of their cars or trucks and sell whatever items are inside. Modern-day artworks, handmade crafts, baked goods, consignments, and services such as palm reading make Renninger's a full-day experience.

As jam-packed as the booths are with shoulder-to-shoulder crowds in winter, die-hard dealers and pickers descend during the periodic, 800-vendor Antiques & Collectors Extravaganzas, a rite-of-passage experience. National Longest Yard Sale events held here are a bargain hunter's delight.

Address 20651 US-441, Mount Dora, FL 32757, +1 (352) 383-3141, www.renningers.net | **Getting there** By car, take US Highway 441 north one mile past its junction with FL-46. The destination is on the right. | **Hours** Fri 10am – 4pm, Sat & Sun 9am – 5pm | **Tip** The Ramsay Building flaunts a gorgeous, wrought-iron balcony that rivals New Orleans' finest. In spite of its exterior glamour, it was once a Piggly Wiggly Grocer (523 N Donnelly Street, Mount Dora).

85 Revolution Adventures
Time to get Mucky

Billing itself as Central Florida's outdoor adventure showcase, Revolution Adventures offers a truly thrilling line-up, from ATV tours to trophy bass fishing. But there is one thing that turns heads and impresses visitors from far and wide: the Mucky Ducks. You'd think amphibious vehicles would be ten a penny in lake-strewn Florida, but, while boating and paddling are certainly popular, this is the only place in the state where you can combine off-roading and motor-boating in the same vehicle.

While only 20 miles from Disney, this Lake County location offers a real break from the theme parks. It's an open-air exercise in motorized fun and non-mechanized challenges, all set in 230 acres of private land with its own lake and multiple trails. The crown jewels are the six-wheel Argo UTVs (Ultimate Terrain Vehicles), aka the Mucky Ducks. These technological marvels are a modern version of World War II's DUKW amphibious trucks that were invariably called Ducks. They are at home both on land and water and therefore ideal for unique, off-road adventures. You can experience them for yourself on Revolution's one-hour tours over the dirt trails and watery elements of this offroad paradise, plunging from dry land to lake and back again, with effortless ease and maximum fun. But they are called "Mucky" for a reason, as you will get muddy. Be sure to wear old clothing.

There are also quad bikes, buggy tours, and jet-skis on offer. Or you can keep your feet firmly on the ground and enjoy target or tag archery, trap shooting, and fishing, with all necessary safety equipment provided. The appeal is to visitors and locals alike, especially since all activities can be customized for team-building and other group events. Feel like shooting the boss in archery tag or proving yourself top dog at clay pigeons? Have a go at it, but remember you'll see those colleagues on Monday.

Address 4000 SR-33, Clermont, FL 34714, +1 (352) 400-1322, www.revolutionoffroad.com | Getting there By car, take East-West Expressway (SR-408) west from downtown to the Florida Turnpike and continue to exit 272, SR-50 west toward Clermont. After 15 miles, turn left onto SR-33. | Hours Daily 8:30am–4:30pm by reservation only | Tip When you want a more sedate outdoor adventure, nearby Lake Louisa State Park provides biking, hiking, boating, and fishing in tranquil surroundings (7305 US-27, Clermont, www.floridastateparks.org/parks-and-trails/lake-louisa-state-park).

86 Rock 'n Roll Heaven

A repository of vinyl veneration

Records were supposed to have died out with the arrival of the CD in the 1980s, but nobody told this humble music store, aptly located in Orlando's Antiques Row district. A local fixture since 1976, it has enjoyed renewed attention in recent times for its extensive record collections, rock 'n roll memorabilia, and staff who could be drawn straight from the Championship Vinyl store in the classic movie *High Fidelity*. But that's to underplay both the staff and astonishing interior of Rock 'n Roll Heaven, a theme park for vinyl junkies.

To walk through the door of this modest venue in an unprepossessing strip mall on Ivanhoe Boulevard is to enter an Aladdin's Cave of music-based nostalgia and homage, a rocking reverence to 60 years of pop culture and creativity. You'll find yourself surrounded by a kaleidoscopic welter of posters, collectibles, T-shirts, toys, and cardboard cut-outs, plus mind-boggling rack upon rack of records that seem to meld into a kind of musical time warp, where the sounds of the 1960s and 1970s are still booming.

What started as a hole-in-the-wall business directly across the street gradually evolved into an ever-expanding space in its current location. It slowly absorbed the businesses on either side in a Tardis-like growth pattern in that the external façade gives no clue to the vast extent inside.

The current custodian of this vinyl veneration is Ray Ehmen, who went from 1980s' collector to owner more than 30 years ago. He sits in splendid supplication at the heart of a record-collecting empire that draws customers from all over the world. He has welcomed a litany of rock titans, from punk rocker Lydia Lunch to The Backstreet Boys, many of whom have left their scrawls on the restroom walls. From the days when you couldn't give records away, Ehmen has seen things come full circle, as mint-condition LPs now command top dollar.

Address 1814 N Orange Avenue, Orlando, FL 32804, +1 (407) 896-1952, www.rock-n-rollheaven.com | Getting there Bus 102 to N Orange Avenue & E New Hampshire Street | Hours Mon–Sat 10am–7:30pm, Sun 11am–4pm | Tip Skateboarders cannot miss Galactic G Skateshop, which offers a huge range of equipment and accessories (2020 N Orange Avenue, www.galacticg.com).

87 __Rogers Kiene Building
Orlando's English heart

When it comes to Orlando's oldest landmarks, few can beat the Rogers Kiene Building, built in 1886 as a gentlemen's club and now home of CityArts. Yet that only hints at the history – and mixed usage – of this notable building's 130-plus years of life.

The arresting, green, two-story edifice with a cupola sits among modern cafés and bars, but when it was built by newly-arrived Englishman Gordon Rogers, it was surrounded by cattle and citrus farms. Known as the English Club, it welcomed a new generation of settlers and an original building style. Not only did it introduce Queen Anne architecture, it debuted a Victorian siding technique typical in Europe but little known in the New World. Look closely at the south and west elevations. Those are extensively pressed zinc, virtually unheard of in the US at the time and imported from Britain by Rogers.

From those early days, the building's occupants changed over the years to include the printing press of the *South Florida Sentinel*, a two-lane bowling alley, and a gathering place for The Puritan Sisterhood of the Dames of Malta and the First Spiritualist Church. It was also a restaurant, dance studio, and locksmith's before falling into disrepair in the 1980s. Happily, businessman and arts benefactor Ford Kiene stepped in with a total renovation in 1999, restoring the pine flooring and iconic forest green paint, and installing his Gallery at Avalon Island and Guinevere's Coffee House, in a nod to the building's heritage. In 2018, Kiene donated it to the city, stipulating only that it be used for the arts, and that paved the way for the boutique galleries and contemporary events of CityArts, with its cute café.

You can still see the underlying lath and plaster in a section of wall Kiene left uncovered as a glimpse into history. Many believe the ghost of Rogers and his wife still keep an eye on the place.

Address 39 S Magnolia Avenue, Orlando, FL 32801, +1 (407) 648-7060, www.downtownartsdistrict.com/cityarts | **Getting there** Bus 60, 62 to N Magnolia Avenue & E Central Boulevard | **Hours** Tue–Sun 11am–6pm | **Tip** For more contemporary art, visit the award-winning photography of Snap! Orlando which includes amazing digital works (420 E Church Street, www.snaporlando.com).

88 Rollins College

Mister Rogers' Winter Park neighborhood

A small college tucked into the southern corner of downtown Winter Park was once the stomping ground of music composition student Fred McFeely Rogers (1928–2003), who would rise to fame as Mister Rogers on the children's television program *Mister Rogers' Neighborhood.*

The show was groundbreaking in many ways, including the manner in which Mister Rogers spoke to children. His natural speech cadence was slow and gentle, which provided a reassuring tone for his young audience, and he never talked down to them. While he was a student in Winter Park, he was active in the Rollins Inter-Faith and Race Relations Committee, and his commitment to racial justice played out in a 1969 episode during which he cooled his feet in a wading pool with the Black character Officer Clemmons. It was a direct stab at the country's segregation of public swimming pools.

Rogers maintained a long relationship with Rollins College, and lasting tributes to him can be found around the campus. At the opening of each *Mister Rogers Neighborhood* episode, Fred put on his iconic sweater, then laced up his sneakers, and these items can be viewed by appointment in the Olin Library. A stone featuring his name, the year he graduated from Rollins College (1951), and the television show's title was placed along the Rollins Walk of Fame in 1991 in front of Frederick Lyman Hall, his former dormitory. *A Beautiful Day for a Neighbor*, a seven-foot-tall, bronze sculpture, memorializes Rogers surrounded by children enthralled with a story he tells through his puppet Daniel Tiger. And a painted portrait of him is located in the Fred Rogers Lobby at the school's John M. Tiedtke Concert Hall. Rogers and fellow Rollins student Anthony Perkins, most famous for his role as Norman Bates in *Psycho*, once performed together at the campus' Annie Russell Theatre in the play *The Madwoman of Chaillot.*

Address 1000 Holt Avenue, Winter Park, FL 32789, +1 (407) 646-2000, www.rollins.edu |
Getting there Bus 443 to E Fairbanks & S Interlachen Avenues | Hours See website for
buildings' hours | Tip As you turn onto Osceola Court from Osceola Avenue, a small, green
sign honoring Fred Rogers reads, *It's a beautiful day in this neighborhood* (Osceola Court,
Winter Park).

89 SAK Comedy Lab
The improv masters

From the Minnesota Renaissance Festival to Orlando is a straight-line journey of 1,547 miles, but it's several lifetimes for an improv comedy group. Yet, that's the origin story of a quirky, quixotic bunch of comedians who inhabit the alternative realm of entertainment where, as they say, "we like to make stuff up."

It has been a distinct laugh-fest ever since four friends got together in Shakopee, Minnesota in 1977 and discovered a love for street theater. Their comic style became sought after at festivals. After a show in Largo, Florida in 1982, they came under the eye of a certain Mouse, or rather, his talent scouts. Invited to perform at Walt Disney World, the SAK Theatre Company, as they were now known, plowed a unique furrow with audience participation during shows around the parks. They honed their quick-witted comedic skills to a fine point.

After their Disney contract expired in 1989, the group opted to stay in Orlando and opened the SAK Comedy Lab in a 99-seat theater on busy Church Street. Among their performers at the time was a young Wayne Brady prior to his going on to be an Emmy-winning comedian in his own right, and Aaron Shure, who would find fame as a writer and producer for *Everyone Loves Raymond* and *The Office*.

Several venue moves, each one to a larger space, and a growing underground following on the nation's comedy circuit have settled SAK as a downtown fixture, with an array of shows and classes. Don't miss their signature improv "Duel of Fools" show in the style of TV's *Whose Line Is It Anyway?* SAK has also produced more talented alumni, such as *Saturday Night Live* writer Paula Pell and Drew Carey sidekick Jonathan Mangum. But mostly they have had a lot of fun and entertained a lot of people, who are happy to see the stuff they make up. The name came from their street theater days, when they kept all their props in a large sack.

Address 55 W Church Street, Suite 211, Orlando, FL 32801, +1 (407) 648-0001, www.sakcomedylab.com | Getting there Bus 3, 7, 11, 13, 15 to S Orange Avenue & W Pine Street | Hours See website for showtimes | Tip Discover more theater-style amusement and quick-witted comedians when you attend a nightly, live-improv murder mystery at Sleuths Mystery Dinner Shows (8267 International Drive, www.sleuths.com).

90 Screamin' Gator Zipline

Gatorland: the park that likes it snappy

Gatorland is a park that's hard to miss, thanks to the giant alligator mouth next to the main entrance. This eye-catching edifice has been its trademark since 1962, nine years before Walt Disney World opened, and it remains an iconic spot in the heart of Florida. Gatorland is also one of the few places in the state where you can legally feed alligators. But just seeing or feeding these reptiles isn't enough for the fun-loving folks behind this family-owned roadside attraction that dates back to 1949. Oh no. They like to give visitors the chance to get closer to the reptile action. Much closer. Like, whizzing over their heads closer. Welcome to the Screamin' Gator Zipline.

This 2011 addition was an instant hit, as it transported intrepid guests on a zipline adventure of epic proportions at heights of 45 to 65 feet and speeds approaching 30 mph. And each zip offers an exclusive perspective on the park's central inhabitants – from directly above. The sequence of five zips and a swinging bridge builds up to the ultimate thrill of traversing the main Breeding Marsh, home to more than 100 hungry alligators. The 500-foot zipline does at least afford its riders the comfort of being 60 feet above the gaping maws, but there is still the intense feeling of being dangled like "gator bait" over the reptile-infested marsh.

Not content with creating such a daunting series of challenges – which can take up to two hours to complete – Gatorland went out on a limb, quite literally, to install the extremely rare zipline designed especially for people with disabilities. At a cost of $500,000, the park's engineers came up with an ingenious system of ramps, harnesses, and electric hoists that allows visitors in wheelchairs to experience the unique thrill of soaring over the mixture of gator ponds and exhibits, proving beyond doubt that courage truly knows no bounds.

And the gators? They're just waitin' around for someone to "drop in" for lunch.

Address 14501 S Orange Blossom Trail, Orlando, FL 32837, +1 (407) 855-5496, www.gatorland.com | Getting there Bus 108 to S Orange Blossom Trail & Cypress Crossing Drive | Hours Daily 10am–5pm | Tip Need more gators? Gatorland has its own 15,000-square-foot Gator Spot reptile oasis within the Fun Spot park just off International Drive (5700 Fun Spot Way, www.fun-spot.com/orlando).

91 Secret Sonar Lab
Orlando's submarine technology base

Inland Orlando, a good 50 miles from the coast, seems a strange choice for a submarine facility. Yet Lake Gem Mary, just south of downtown, played a pivotal role in sonar research to aid the US Navy's underwater fleet for more than 50 years.

Established in 1941 as a makeshift unit operated by Columbia University's Division of War Research, the facility calibrated and tested sonar transducers for underwater detection. The lake was chosen for its ideal underwater profile: round and conical, with a sound-absorbent floor. In 1945, the Navy took it over. Six years later, as the Cold War heated up, it was dramatically expanded as the Underwater Sound Reference Division of the Naval Research Laboratory, with an extensive array of facilities, including a large, steel pier and a variety of tubes and tanks that could simulate water depths up to three-and-a-half miles.

The hush-hush lab was at the forefront of helping to develop silent-running American submarines while refining detection systems for Soviet subs. The high-tech facility was home to experts in sonar physics and engineering. Its budget had reached $12 million a year by 1988, and it continued to exist in this quiet residential area until a 1997 shutdown. While there was always an air of secrecy over the lakeside site, there were also wild rumors of what was there, including the suggestion of an underground tunnel to the sea. But the lake was only 33 feet deep, and the stories were easily debunked.

Orange County schools took over the main building, and it existed as Fort Gatlin Administrative Center for several years before being abandoned again in 2022. Fort Gatlin? Yes, this was the site of Orlando's original permanent structure in 1838, part of the Second Seminole Wars. The secret sonar lab building and the historic marker for Fort Gatlin now sit on the deserted site, testament to not one but two bygone ages.

Address 3909 Summerlin Avenue, Orlando, FL 32806 | Getting there By car, from I-4, take exit 80 south on Orange Blossom Trail (US 17-92), turn left onto Holden Avenue, right onto S Orange Avenue, and left onto Gatlin Avenue | Hours Unrestricted | Tip Just a few blocks away is a small marker for The Council Oak, traditional meeting place of the Indian chiefs in the Second Seminole War (4505 S Ferncreek Avenue).

92 Showcase of Citrus
Orlando P. D. or Pre-Disney

If you'd like to know what Lake County looked like before The Mouse moved to Florida, head to Highway 27 and visit Showcase of Citrus. Prior to Disney's arrival, this part of Central Florida was totally agricultural, consisting purely of mile after mile of citrus groves. Even after the Magic Kingdom opened, this area remained comfortably detached, only 20-odd miles from the theme parks but light years away in culture and lifestyle. Mickey and Co. did their thing, and the citrus farmers did theirs.

But then came the orange-killing freezes of the 1980s, along with a boom in vacation homes. Highway 27 was transformed into a sprawling dormitory town, an adjunct to the mighty tourist machine across the county line. But the Arnold family still believed in citrus. While most groves were bulldozed wholesale to create communities of gated "villas," a lone business stubbornly bucked the trend. Starting out in 1989 as a humble roadside shack, Showcase of Citrus forged an alternative, retro path, offering little more than the chance to pick fresh oranges and savor the taste of fruit that hadn't been sprayed with fertilizers or artificial substances to make it look ripe.

And a funny thing happened as a result. Many of those visiting tourists decided the low-tech world of citrus was still appealing, and the simple pleasures of fruit-picking and a country store were an attraction in their own right. Suitably encouraged, the Arnold family added a petting zoo and monster truck tours of their 2,500-acre property, along with a magic ingredient: delicious orange slushies and fresh mimosas made from their own fruit.

Today, savvy locals know when to visit to get the freshest seasonal produce, including the various types of tangerines, Persian limes, kumquats and trademark oranges, while tourists enjoy kicking back on the front porch of the store and saying hello to Joe the camel!

Address 15051 Frank Jarrell Road, Clermont, FL 34714, +1 (352) 394-4377, www.showcaseofcitrus.com | **Getting there** By car, from I-4 W take exit 64 for US-192 west and continue eight miles to US-27. Turn right for US-27 north and continue five miles to the destination. | **Hours** Daily 9am–7pm | **Tip** For more tastes of yesteryear, visit historic Webb's Candy Shop, offering citrus candies, goats milk fudge, and hand-dipped chocolates since 1932 (38217 US-27, www.webbscandyshop.com).

93 Simply Cheese
Cheese Board 101

The mark of a good host or hostess is their ability to create dishes that are as visually appealing as they are tasty, making a good impression on their guests from appetizers to desserts. The Simply Cheese shop in Winter Park offers one-hour Cheese Board 101 classes that pair hands-on instruction for assembling a gorgeous cheese and charcuterie board with one or two bottles of wine per group, ensuring a convivial afternoon's lesson.

Ann Thornton, owner of Simply Cheese, had a brainstorm during a vacation in Grand Rapids, Michigan with her husband Kyle and their children. The COVID-19 pandemic laid waste to her job in medical sales, and she was looking for a new direction. Standing in a cheese shop during that family get-away, she decided that was the path for her, and upon their return home she and Kyle set out to make the dream a reality. Two years and a lot of hard work later, they opened Simply Cheese in Winter Park.

In time, the shop added classes to its offerings, including Cheese Board 101, which educates participants in the art of creating a beautiful platter of cheeses, meats, fruit, crackers, and spreads that is as appealing to the eye as it is delicious when devoured. The ethos is simple: if it's just you and a friend or loved one, slap a hearty chunk of cheese on a plate, add some crackers, and dig in, no classes required. If you intend to make a splash with your culinary prowess while entertaining, however, it's time to learn some basic skills, and Cheese Board 101 is just the way to do it. Like all good parties that include cheese and nibbly bits, wine is part of the 90-minute class experience, as are games and a lot of laughter. Reservations are required, as are a minimum of eight guests for each class, though they don't all have to come from the same group so it's a chance to meet new friends while creating beautiful and deliciously edible masterpieces.

Address 2258 Aloma Avenue, Winter Park, FL 32792, +1 (321) 972-6186, www.simplycheesefl.com | Getting there Bus 13 to Aloma Avenue & Strathy Lane | Hours Tue–Fri 11am–7pm, Sat 10am–4pm, see website for class schedule | Tip Just across Aloma Avenue is Sprouts Market, where you can pick up fresh fruit and other gourmet treats to go with your home-crafted charcuterie board (1989 Aloma Avenue, Winter Park, www.sprouts.com).

94 Sinkhole at Lake Rose

Winter Park's house-eating hole

A collection of catastrophes lies beneath the glittering waters of Lake Rose, situated on the corner of Fairbanks Avenue and Denning Drive. Winter Park resident Mae Rose Owen's three-bedroom house, a selection of luxury vehicles, sections of two roads, a truck camper, and a swimming pool were all swallowed up by what became one of Florida's largest sinkholes.

In 1981, the ground beneath Mae Rose's property sucked down a few trees before she realized something unstoppable was happening. According to news sources, she grabbed her dog Muffin, whatever personal property she could remove quickly, and fled the impending disaster. Within 48 hours, everything she couldn't remove was gone, having dropped into a hole that eventually expanded to 350 feet wide.

The back end of a local luxury car dealership became one with the land's erosion, and a handful of its Porsches went with it, only a few of which were ever recovered. Winter Park also lost part of its Olympic-sized community swimming pool to the great gobbling ground. The only thing gentle about the event was the way the gradual, sloped sides of the sinkhole reached down to the deep central pit.

While the crater was a tragedy for those who lost property, the small gain that came from it was a greater understanding of what causes sinkholes. Contrary to popular belief, it wasn't dry conditions that led to these massive land drops, said geologist Jim Jammal, expert on the subject and the City of Winter Park's engineer, who was tasked with studying Florida's newest bowl of utter destruction. Instead, he discovered, heavy rainfall after a period of drought was a major factor in their formation.

Today, the 75-foot-deep lake that formed from the sinkhole is named after the unfortunate Mae Rose. It has been stabilized with sand and concrete to provide enjoyment for a lucky new batch of waterfront-property homeowners.

Address 900 W Comstock Avenue, Winter Garden, FL 32789 | Getting there Bus 9, 23 to S Denning Drive & W Comstock Avenue | Hours Unrestricted | Tip In 2015, a sinkhole reopened on Groveland's S Iowa Avenue. After being refilled, the driveway that collapsed appears stable – for now (524 E Waldo Street, Groveland).

95__Steinmetz Hall
Acoustic perfection in a transforming hall

Steinmetz concert hall inside the $550 million Dr. Phillips Center for the Performing Arts offers a stunning aural experience. One of the world's most acoustically perfect venues with or without amplification, it earned an N1 sound rating, which refers to the lowest possible sound the human ear can detect. That accolade comes through perfectly loud and unforgettably clear during performances.

The theater's concrete walls, "floating" concrete base, and the rubber pads it was built on offer a separation of sorts from the rooms around it, helping to dampen any noise intrusion from the adjoining theaters and from outside traffic. Designers applied vibration and noise reducing measures to the air conditioning, plumbing, and even the lighting. Wood and cork flooring add another layer of noise dampening, while other elements work towards transmitting and reflecting sound. Every decision having to do with optimum acoustical enjoyment was considered, and these efforts are invisible to audience members, who simply enjoy a perfect theatrical experience.

Steinmetz Hall is also an expert "transformer." Its stage and the hall's walls can be made longer or shorter, as can the floor, which features specially built chairs that rise up from or rotate under the floor to accommodate audiences ranging from 1,597 to a maximum of 1,741. During the process of raising the seats from beneath wooden flooring, they rotate upward and forward, and what was flat flooring becomes rows on which guests can walk.

The unique, multi-form theater's lush, cherry-wood interior walls are encased in a movable concrete frame, too, taking it from a square space with traditional rows of orchestra-level seating to rounded proscenium style with four levels of crescent seating, ensuring there isn't a bad seat in the house for the concerts, presentations, plays, and musicals you'll enjoy there.

Address 445 S Magnolia Avenue, Orlando, FL 32801, +1 (407) 358-6603, www.drphillipscenter.org | **Getting there** Bus 3, 13, 15, 61 to E Anderson Street & S Magnolia Avenue | **Hours** See website for showtimes | **Tip** On a more intimate scale, Orlando Shakespeare Theater, known locally as Orlando Shakes, produces classic and family-friendly shows (812 E Rollins Street, www.orlandoshakes.org).

96__Studio K
The graceful art of lightsaber combat

Not everyone loves to dance, so Studio K found a way to blend dance-like movement with *Star Wars* fanaticism through their Lightsaber Technique classes designed to tap into your inner Jedi – or bring out your Dark Side – during one-hour workouts featuring choreographed "fighting."

Having worked for such prestigious companies as the Miss America Organization, Give Kids The World, and Orlando's Full Sail University, Kristin Weissman knew what it took to bring that "something extra" when she founded Studio K in 2010 and created "the studio where pop culture meets dance and fitness." But there was a bigger goal, too: she wanted a place where adults could get fit while enjoying dance without joining a kid-oriented class.

In 2018, Mandy Shroyer-Patino arrived, with eight years of experience on the Renaissance Faire circuit, including hand-to-hand combat and fighting with short swords, daggers, staffs, and shields. After *Star Wars: The Force Awakens* premiered in 2015, Shroyer-Patino had shifted her focus to lightsaber training. Once she introduced her fitness-oriented lightsaber lessons to Studio K, the classes quickly became popular. Over time, she added battle moves and their artistic use in film choreography to the class, blending her love of *Star Wars* with her passion for stage combat.

Depending on your comfort level and experience, you'll go to a beginning or intermediate/advanced group, and that's when the fun of creating lightsaber choreography starts. You'll warm-up, practice the basics of proper footwork and form, and then learn a series of attack and defense moves.

Don't worry if things feel new to you. Most humans weren't raised the way Jedi younglings are and have no real experience welding a lightsaber. So no one is going to judge you as you hone your warrior skills. Studio K supplies lightsabers if you don't have your own.

The floor is yours!™

Address 11951 International Drive South, Units 2A3 & 2A4, Orlando, FL 32821, +1 (407) 778-4607, www.studiokorlando.com | **Getting there** Bus 8 to International Drive & Riveroaks Bay Drive | **Hours** Mon–Fri 6:30–9:30pm, see website for class times | **Tip** Martial Arts combine with Brazilian dance at Capoeira Brazilian Pelourinho, through fun lessons for all ages (7075 Kingspointe Parkway, Unit 10, www.capoeirabrazilpelo.com).

97 Super Awesome Cool Pottery

Clay throwing for kids

Children have a natural affinity for art, and the pursuit is even better when it comes with the chance to stick their fingers into soft, squishy clay and come out of it with a bowl they've made themselves. While many art studios offer paint-your-own ceramics classes, Super Awesome Cool Pottery goes one step further and allows budding crafters ages 5 – 17 (along with their grown-ups) to throw their own hand-crafted bowl on a potter's wheel during two-hour, privately-reserved Family Potter's Wheel classes. Experienced artists guide the students and teach them pottery techniques during the class.

Up to six people at a time can take the class, and each one must sign up individually for a given time slot. On the day of the session, a staff member will provide the necessary instructions, and then it's off to the pottery wheels for an hour of fun-filled clay throwing. During the class, the participants will mold their wet clay, coaxing it outward and upward until it transforms into a bowl. Time is allowed for each bowl to partially dry, after which budding potters can paint their creation in whatever colors or designs speak to their inner artist. The bowls are then allowed to dry fully for a week before they're fired in a kiln to bring out their beauty. You can pick up the finished masterpiece at the studio when the studio notifies you that it's ready, or you can make prior arrangements for it to be delivered to your home. Super Awesome Cool Pottery offers the same class for adults only, during which participants will create two bowls.

In addition to the Family Potter's Wheel classes, youngsters and their adults can try hand-building with clay, turning an idea into a masterpiece with the help of an artist, or choose a pre-made piece to paint. It will then be fired and ready for pick-up once it has cooled. Pottery is messy work, so wear clothes that can get muddy.

thoughts are whi...
...tter's wheel; I k...
...am nor what I de...
—W...

Address 930 Hoffner Avenue, Orlando, FL 32809, +1 (407) 720-3699,
www.superawesomecool.com, studio@superawesomecool.com | Getting there Bus 7,
11, 18 to Hansel & Hoffner Avenues | Hours Tue & Wed 10am–6pm, Thu–Mon
10am–8pm | Tip Kids can further tap into their artistic side while having fun through
more than 20 activities at the massive Crayola Experience (8001 S Orange Blossom Trail,
www.crayolaexperience.com).

98 Tank America

Where you really can crush it

"Hey, did you know we can buy tanks?" When a phone call starts like that, you know there's going to be some serious follow-up. The answer to the query was clearly, "Let's do it!" because Tank America is now firmly cemented among Orlando's unlikely but irresistible attractions. Come here if you want to drive a genuine ex-Army tank and crush cars with it.

The call was between business partners Troy Lotane and John Kinney, and it was the catalyst for their unique tank-driving experience. They started in Melbourne, Florida, but when the COVID-19 pandemic forced them to reassess, they moved to this 14-acre site in Orlando that replicates battlefield conditions. Neither had any tank expertise, although Troy had served in the Navy. So they recruited a team of veterans to provide expertise and authenticity for their intense playground. They initially bought three 17-ton British Rolls-Royce-powered FV433 Abbott tanks from the 1960s and refitted them with engines for which they can actually get spare parts today.

The battlefield they created comes with a jungle section, a 75-foot-long mud ditch, hills, and trenches, plus scrap cars that can be crushed into oblivion. The main course is a half-mile long, and everyone gets to drive it twice. There's also the "Combat Locked" option of driving with all hatches closed, just like being in real combat.

The guns don't fire, of course, but it is still an ultra-realistic exercise. The inventory has grown to include six Abbotts plus three armored personnel carriers (APCs), all maintained by ex-Army and Navy personnel who revel in the role of instructors. On a busy week, they will trash around 25 old cars, and the tanks roll come rain or shine. You'll drive as the instructor sits on the tank's hull to one side of you, connected via intercom. For spectators, it is thrilling enough. For drivers, well, Tank America really crushes it.

Address 6605 Muskogee Street, Orlando, FL 32807, +1 (407) 213-8265, www.tankamerica.com | Getting there By car, from I-4 E take exit 84B for Colonial Drive. Turn right onto E Colonial Drive, continue for five miles and turn right onto Old Cheney Highway, left onto Forsyth Road, and left on Muskogee Street. | Hours Thu–Mon 10am–4pm by reservation only | Tip After your ground-based fun, take to the skies with Air Force Fun helicopter tours from their International Drive heliport (5525 International Drive, www.airforcefun.com).

99 __ Ted Bundy Trial
A serial killer's day of reckoning

Charming and handsome, Theodore Robert Bundy's charisma didn't save him from execution. One of the nation's most heinous serial killers, Bundy's trial for the 1978 murder of 12-year-old schoolgirl Kimberly Leach was held in February 1980 in what was then the annex of the Orange County Courthouse, now the Heritage Square Park courtyard in front of the Orange County Regional History Center. The courtyard was created when the annex was torn down due to asbestos, and it's chilling to think that this monster once stood on this very spot.

In a shocking turn of events during his trial, Bundy, acting as his own attorney, was taking the testimony of his girlfriend Carol Ann Boone, when he abruptly said, "Do you want to marry me?" Under oath and in the presence of the judge, she replied, "Yes." Bundy elicited further testimony from her confirming she was aware of his desire to marry her. He declared their nuptials complete, and a legally binding marriage license was stamped by a notary public, whose presence Boone had arranged earlier.

After more than seven hours of deliberation that same day, the jurors were unanimous: Ted Bundy was found guilty of kidnapping and first-degree murder, and at his sentencing the recommendation was "Death." The Orlando trial wasn't the first time Bundy had been sentenced to death, though. The same year he brutally took Kimberly Leach's life, he also killed Florida State University sorority sisters Margaret Bowman and Lisa Levy. During the July 24, 1979 trial in Miami, he was sentenced to death for their murders.

After 10 years on death row, Bundy met his grisly end on January 24, 1989 in the electric chair at the Florida State Prison, having confessed on tape during his final days in prison to 30 murders across five states. His body was cremated, and it is believed his ashes were dispersed in Washington's Cascade Mountains.

Address 65 E Central Boulevard, Orlando, FL 32801, +1 (407) 836-8500, www.thehistorycenter.org | **Getting there** Bus 60, 62 to N Magnolia Avenue & E Central Boulevard | **Hours** Mon–Sat 10am–5pm, Sun noon–5pm | **Tip** If you need to balance your own chakras, or you'd simply like some nice spices and relaxing teas, visit Mystic Minerals Metaphysical Herb Shop (4809 S Orange Avenue, www.mysticmineralsmarket.com).

100_ Tibet-Butler Preserve

The unexpected sounds of Walt Disney World

Orlando's zip codes have expanded far west of the downtown area, and as the city has grown, many natural areas have been overtaken. But 21 miles beyond the urban core and 4 miles from the manic pace of Walt Disney World is a 440-acre natural refuge with hiking trails and activities for all fitness levels. Nestled into a wooded area off Winter Garden-Vineland Road, this sleepy little gem sits in the most unexpected of places, surrounded by the bustle of modern life.

The preserve offers family-friendly eco programs, and the Vera Carter Environmental Center hosts information and displays about animals. You can enjoy a series of six interconnected hiking trails, from the 0.11-mile Screech Owl Trail – just long enough to stretch your legs – to the 1.08-mile Palmetto Passage, which gives experienced hikers a look at pine flatwoods, mixed forest wetlands, and bay swamps. Combine the Fallen Log Crossing and Osprey Overlook trails for a nearly two-mile-round-trip hike to scenic Lake Tibet-Butler, where a covered overlook provides shelter from the sun, plus a stunning view. This is swamp land, so be aware that the trails may be muddy after it rains.

Among the center's wild residents are armadillos, gopher tortoises, snakes, alligators, racoons, river otters, and a host of birdlife, including woodpeckers, wild turkeys, bald eagles, and other raptors. You can use the preserve's trail book to record the wildlife you observed during your hike. But one of the lesser-known experiences during your visit to Tibet-Butler is the sounds of ferry boat horns, train whistles, and, if the wind is in the right direction, music from parades and live shows, all of which emanate from the Walt Disney World theme parks and waterways. It's a surprising addition to an afternoon hike in a natural setting. You'll feel the exciting Disney vibe while feeling light years away from it all.

Predators in the Sky
During a hike, it is easy to overlook the wildlife in the sky. Look up! The preserve is home to many birds of prey such as hawks, vultures, ospreys, and eagles. These birds help fight overpopulation and disease by preying on animals such as rats, mice, rabbits, fish, carrion (dead animals), and other birds. During your hike, don't forget to look up and enjoy these graceful hunters.

Address 8777 Winter Garden-Vineland Road, Orlando, FL 32836, +1 (407) 254-1940, www.orangecountyfl.net/CultureParks/Parks.aspx | Getting there By car, from I-4 W take exit 68 and turn right onto S Apopka Vineland Road. Turn left onto Winter Garden-Vineland Road and drive 5.6 miles to the destination. | Hours Daily 8am–6pm | Tip Avid birders can spot more than 220 species at Orlando Wetlands Park, including the rare-to-Florida purple martin in springtime (25155 Wheeler Road, Christmas, www.orlando.gov/Parks-the-Environment/Directory/Wetlands-Park).

101 Timucua Arts Foundation
Live from the living room

If you have ever wondered what it would be like to have a wonderful concert in the comfort of your living room, wonder no more. The extraordinary Glazer family had that thought too and turned it into reality. The family's Timucua Arts Foundation stages around 100 concerts a year in their South Downtown home. Okay, it's not your average living room, but Benoit Glazer and wife Elaine Corriveau, along with their children, have created a fabulously original venue for live jazz, chamber music, swing, and experimental projects.

The family believes that art and music belong to everyone, as they are the highest manifestation of humanity and should be best enjoyed in the intimate confines of the living room. And the family members live what they preach. It all started in September, 2000, when Glazer, who was then the musical director for the Cirque du Soleil company in Walt Disney World, couldn't find the kind of music he wanted to hear on his nights off. So he and Corriveau staged their own concerts. At home.

Squeezing 40 guests into their modest abode worked on a limited basis, but the couple soon realized they had to think bigger. The solution was to build a new house that just happened to include a cozy, 100-seat concert hall, a living room with real elbow room, and outstanding acoustics. It opened in August, 2007, and now The White House, as it's known due to its monochromatic exterior, has become a true Bohemian arthouse.

Named for the original Indigenous Americans who once lived in the region, the foundation operates three programs: an Open House – pay what you want, bring wine to share; Live at Timucua – well-priced tickets for genuine master musicians; and WordPlay – theater, film, poetry, and literary events. Sample any of them, and you will discover a unique musical experience presented by people who genuinely open their hearts and their home to the arts.

Address 2000 S Summerlin Avenue, Orlando, FL 32806, +1 (321) 234-3985, www.timucua.com | Getting there Bus 3 to Delaney Avenue & Kaley Street | Hours See website for performance schedule | Tip For the latest Cirque du Soleil performance, head to Disney Springs, where the breathtaking "Drawn to Life" is on stage twice a night, Tuesdays through Saturdays (Lake Buena Vista, www.cirquedusoleil.com/drawn-to-life).

102 __ The Traveler
Orlando Airport's stationary resident

When it comes to travelers, Orlando International Airport (OIA) sees more than most. Florida's top air gateway typically ranks in the country's top 10, hosting around 50 million passengers a year. But OIA – or MCO, as it is known from its international code, thanks to its previous life as McCoy Air Force Base – has one traveler who never leaves the concourse and is the subject of much viral debate.

Located adjacent to the main Food Court, the weary figure taking a nap next to his bags has remained a constant since 1985, when *The Traveler* was unveiled. The figure is, of course, a life-size, hyper-realistic sculpture, part of the airport's extensive investment in art. Created by artist Duane Hanson, cast in bronze, polychromed in oil, with baggage, the artwork has become a much-loved focal point. Dressed in blue shorts, pink polo shirt, and running shoes, the 250-pound sculpture sits with one leg extended, and his head is supported by his right hand, propped on two flight bags. Hanson employed painstaking touches to achieve the illusion, such as using human hair on the head and mustache. He also staged a clever stunt at the work's unveiling. The model for the piece was his real-life neighbor, who was quietly in attendance. Posing next to the sculpture and seemingly a part of it, he abruptly stood up and walked away, throwing the audience into startled amusement.

The Traveler has required several refurbishments over the years due to interactions with passengers, including some who threw coins at him for good luck. While the interaction was appreciated, the work was eventually encased in acrylic in its current location, where he continues to delight and intrigue passengers. A TikTok user started their own tale of confusion in 2021 with a video of the sleepy figure and the challenge, "Is he real?" The video topped 300,000 views in just a few months.

Address 1 Jeff Fuqua Boulevard, Orlando, FL 32827, www.orlandoairports.net | Getting there SunRail to Sand Lake Road; bus 11, 42, 51, 111 to Orlando International Airport | Hours Unrestricted | Tip MCO's other iconic site is B-52 Memorial Park, a homage to the airport's days as a US Air Force base, which features a retired B-52D Stratofortress (8100 Bear Road).

The Traveler
Duane Hanson (1925-1996)
Bronze, polychromed in oil,
mixed media with accessories,
1983

103 __ Truist Plaza

An outdoor room with a view

Downtown's skyline added another towering skyscraper to its portfolio of interesting edifices in 2019 with the opening of the Truist Plaza, a 28-story colossus that impresses with its architecture, high-tech features, and a lofty outdoor overview of the city.

The lower section of the building is impressive enough, mixing nine floors for parking with offices and retail, as well as incorporating access to the SunRail commuter rail service. But the distinct upper portion is where it takes on a different dimension with a color contrast that picks out the dramatic, stepped profile and double-height, open terrace two-thirds of the way up. The top 10 floors are given over to the Marriott's AC Hotel, including the gorgeous Sky Bar roof terrace, with breathtaking vistas to the West and South. You can take the express elevator straight to the 18th floor, cross the lobby lounge, and soak up the dazzling, al fresco views that extend for 120 degrees around the terrace. Just make sure you have your sunglasses firmly in hand as you push through the dark-tinted glass door.

The immediate vista is directly to the West and incorporates a gorgeous, practically straight-line overlook of Orlando's three big sporting venues: the Amway Center – home of the NBA's Orlando Magic; INTER&Co Stadium for soccer teams Orlando City and Orlando Pride; and Camping World Stadium, which stages annual College Bowl football games. Then, to the Southwest, those with keen vision (or binoculars) can make out the distinctive high-rise elements of Universal Orlando, notably Volcano Bay and the sleek, 17-story Aventura Hotel. Sky Bar boasts one of downtown's most distinctive vantage points, and you can enhance the experience even more with a drink from the outdoor bar. The gin-infused Cloud is a favorite. Or, better yet, come here for the signature Sunday Brunch with seasonal themes.

Address 333 S Garland Avenue, Orlando, FL 32801, +1 (407) 635-2300, www.acskybar.com | Getting there SunRail to Church Street; bus 61, 62 to W South Street & Boone Avenue | Hours Mon 4–11pm, Tue–Thu & Sun 11am–11pm, Fri & Sat 11am–midnight | Tip Another great rooftop hot-spot is Universal's Bar 17 Bistro atop its Aventura Hotel, which offers superb views over the International Drive area (6725 Adventure Way, www.universalorlando.com).

104__UCF Arboretum

A rare treat along the university's nature trails

College kids aren't the only ones who need to de-stress from too much brain activity and not enough fresh air. Most of us need to take some deep breaths more often than we do. So, to fill the need for more time spent in nature, the University of Central Florida (UCF) Arboretum has carved out a massive complex of hiking trails that traverse distinctly Floridian habitats.

With a bit of luck, your keen eyes will spot a rare subspecies of *Sporobolus floridanus* grass, found only in select locations in northeast and central Florida. Thanks to UCF's controlled burns, *Sporobolus osceolensis*, a type of perennial dropseed grass whose flowering is stimulated by human-made and lightning-strike fires, also makes its home here. Look for grasses with delicate seed heads that look like tiny pockets of fog from a distance. Along with nearly 50 species of birds, hikers may also see white tailed deer, racoons, rabbits, moles, and other mammals, plus reptiles, including turtles and snakes.

There are three sets of trails on 83 acres that add up to a total of 14 miles of hiking. Arboretum trails offer five loops that traverse marshes, wet prairie, flatwoods, and swamp, while the remote East Parcel trails highlight various flatwoods, swamps, and mesic hammock evergreens. On the north-west side of campus, Lake Claire's three loops are home to scrub and forest wetlands. Regardless of which trail system you choose, pack lunch or a snack and plenty of water. Each has a loop with a picnic table for enjoying the sounds of nature.

UCF offers three inexpensive guided tours: the Arboretum Tour and Natural Lands Tour, which run 60 to 90 minutes, and the 3.5-hour Best of Both Worlds Tour. You may prefer to set out on a free, self-guided tour. Be sure to keep an eye out for near-sighted armadillos. Did you know that they can jump five feet straight up when startled!

Address 4312 Scorpius Street, Orlando, FL 32816, www.arboretum.ucf.edu, arboretum@ucf.edu | Getting there By car, take the East-West Expressway (SR-408) to the Central Florida GreeneWay (417 north), then to exit 37A. Turn right onto University Boulevard, right onto Gemini Boulevard S, and left onto Scorpius Street. | Hours Daily dawn–dusk, guided tours Mon–Fri 8am–4pm | Tip Release your inner warrior with a sunset visit to University of Central Florida, where a storm drain in a gully near the Arboretum houses thousands of bats (4312 Scorpius Street, www.arboretum.ucf.edu).

105__ Vault 5421

Gods & Monsters' answer to the apocalypse

What starts as a shop packed with comic books, games, and all manner of "nerd-ware" suddenly morphs into a post-apocalyptic bar with barely an inch of wall or ceiling space left untouched by creepy pop-culture and horror-movie-inspired props. Vault 5421, named for the store's street address, is tucked into a back corner of the venue, offering a semi-darkened "wasteland," where guests can imbibe their chosen libation in an ominous ambiance.

Inspired by their previous space-port style bar Offworld Lounge, Anna Young, the owner of Gods & Monsters, and her husband Todd Fisher tapped into the vibe of *Mad Max* and the post-apocalyptic movie genre they love to create Vault 5421. They decorated it with found objects, items they collected while dumpster-diving, and junk from construction sites, as well as creatures from their own collections and those of friends. Two key designers on the project were experienced fabricators, who did contract work for Disney and Universal. In the end, 90 percent of the bar was made by hand.

Among the Vault's most notable props are a 20-foot-tall skeleton wearing a gas mask, a caged "child" wearing bunny slippers and holding a teddy bear, and a pod creature that looks like its last meal was found sitting at the nearby VIP booth. Up in a corner lurks the life-sized head of the Xenomorph from the movie *Aliens*, which Todd helped create. Cosplay is highly encouraged, as is an attitude of inclusiveness. And rest assured that you won't be the only one to dress up. People drop in dressed as their favorite character just to pick up their comic books, let alone enter the bar. Visit during events, such as the annual Vampire Ball, when cosplayers turn out in droves.

Encouragement is part of the shop's ethos too. When fans say they'd like to do something similar, Todd enthuses, "You should do it. Right now. Go get a loan and put something together!"

Address 5421 International Drive, Orlando, FL 32819, +1 (407) 270-6273,
www.godmonsters.com | Getting there Bus 8, 42 to International & Municipal Drives |
Hours Wed & Thu 5 – 11pm, Fri 5pm – 12:50am, Sat 3pm – 12:50am | Tip Look the part
while surviving a zombie apocalypse with an outfit from the American Army & Navy
surplus store (6210 S Orange Blossom Trail).

106 Washburn Imports

The antique store with Disney appeal

Orlando's Antiques Row is aptly named for its eclectic stores dealing in vintage furniture, art, and bric-a-brac. But undoubtedly the most impressive is Washburn Imports. This former Art Deco warehouse took on its role of importer-in-chief in 1997 after owner John Washburn paid a visit to Indonesia, where a surfing buddy got him hooked on the local artisan furniture.

From one initial 20-foot shipping container, Washburn quickly became renowned for acquiring exotic goods from all over Southeast Asia, notably India, Vietnam, Thailand, and Myanmar, as well as Indonesia. Word of his unique import business quickly spread, and before long, Disney and the other theme parks were beating a path to his door. On one occasion, Busch Gardens in Tampa bought a full-size motorized *tuk tuk* for their *Pantopia* area, while Universal snapped up a number of small accessories and accent pieces for their *Wizarding Worlds of Harry Potter*. Disney bought a variety of Indian chests that found their way into the *Pirates of the Caribbean* ride.

Washburn and managing partner Paul Jones now chart regular passages to the Far East, returning with 40-foot containers packed with furniture and other curiosities that give their store a genuine Aladdin's Cave vibe. They have customers who are anxious to see the latest pieces as soon as the delivery trucks arrive. As Jones says, "It is constantly changing whenever a container comes. It is like a whole new store the next day."

The dynamic duo even found a novel way to survive the 2008 financial crisis. With Washburn's background in bar and restaurant management, they turned one room of the store into an eclectic cocktail lounge to create a new revenue stream. It was such a hit that it's now a full-time business: part antique showroom, part bar. So, if you like the furniture you're sitting on while you sip, you can buy it and take it home with you.

Address 1800 N Orange Avenue, Orlando, FL 32804, +1 (407) 228-4403, www.washburnimports.com | Getting there Bus 102 to N Orange Avenue & E New Hampshire Street | Hours Mon–Sat 11am–6pm, Sun noon–5pm | Tip For more authentic exotic furniture and hand-made home goods, check out Living Morocco just one block north (1804 N Orange Avenue, www.living-morocco-online.com).

107 — Wave Hotel

Lake Nona's artistic "living room"

You might think a hotel loaded with high-tech features, like a robot server, smart toilets, and self-tinting windows, would be an attraction in its own right, but Lake Nona's Wave Hotel goes beyond the confines of chic hospitality. Way beyond. In fact, this unique masterpiece by international investors at the Tavistock Group, developers of the Lake Nona area, is really a well-disguised work of art.

The 17-story edifice is instantly notable for its wave-like profile featuring architectural trickery that gives the building the look of sinuous, blue-glass towers. Even the parking garage matches the styling. Filipino American artist Jefrë created a visual version of braille in circular cut-outs with LED lighting for a signature nighttime look.

As you enter what is nominally the lobby, the space defies the usual definition of a hotel's most functional area. It's called the Living Room and is billed as a facility for local residents and paying guests alike. It includes more than 300 pieces of art in a madcap setting of lighting and imagination, including a two-story, pink dogwood tree. Food and drinks are equally inventive, with that same tech-meets-art vibe, including the show-stopping, Michelin-recognized restaurant Bacàn, featuring a digital mural of Greek goddess Gaia. Don't be surprised to meet Rosie, a robot busser, who can deliver cocktails and small plates to your table.

But all the high-tech elements pale beside the stunning tableau that is the outdoor sculpture garden. This 50,000-square-foot outdoor art gallery is shaded by palm trees and tropical plants, and sprinkled with famous sculptures worth multi-millions. Many of them are from the private collection of Tavistock's owner Joe Lewis, including the twin of Arturo Di Modica's Wall Street icon *Charging Bull* and two pieces by Henry Moore. Lights and lasers add extra razzle-dazzle after dark for a scene that is utterly captivating.

Address 6100 Wave Hotel Drive, Orlando, FL 32827, +1 (407) 675-2000, www.lakenonawavehotel.com | Getting there By car, take the Central Florida GreeneWay (417) to exit 19 and go south on Lake Nona Boulevard. Turn right on Nemours Parkway, then left on Wave Hotel Drive. | Hours Unrestricted | Tip For more high-tech artistry, see The Beacon & Code Wall at the heart of Lake Nona Town Center, which comes to life in dichroic glass with video and music (6943 Lake Nona Boulevard, www.lakenona.com/thing/the-beacon-code-wall).

108 Wekiva Island

The sustainable and rural paddling oasis

Florida is famous for its natural springs and the crystal-clear rivers that issue from them. While Orlando urbanites might think they need to travel a fair distance to enjoy these charms, there is a spring tucked away just 15 miles from the heart of downtown. Five-acre Wekiva Island was established in 2008 with the aim of proving that a sustainable business can be both successful and carbon neutral. You can come here for a rustic rural retreat, with all manner of paddling opportunities on the scenic, spring-fed Wekiva River.

The site of a former fishing camp and restaurant popular with 1940s and 1950s cowboy star Roy Rogers, among others, the island was the victim of several fires over the years, and rebuilding was done in a sympathetic style to suit its tranquil location each time. Have a drink at the Tooting Otter Bar or a bite at Without A Paddle Café, the resident food truck. The General Store offers essential creature comforts, while there are rentals for lounge chairs, cabanas, canoes, kayaks, and paddleboards to explore the pristine, 16-mile waterway, one of Florida's two nationally designated Scenic and Wild Rivers and encompassed by lush, tropical forest.

The Weinaug family bought the Wekiva Marina in 2008, and they have added an arts and education center to boost their environmentally friendly mission for Wekiva Island. Solar power, recycling, rainwater reuse, and water conservation are all part of their patented CERO program that stands for Conservation, Efficiency, Renewables, and Offsets.

The weekends see live music at the Tooting Otter, which makes for a relaxing date night, while periodic events include Holiday specials, notably for Christmas, when they stage a Winter Wonderland spectacular complete with Mr. and Mrs. Claus and a 30-foot Christmas tree. It's hard to beat this outdoor venue where you can enjoy a cool drink surrounded by Mother Nature.

Address 1014 Miami Springs Drive, Longwood, FL 32779, +1 (407) 862-1500, www.wekivaisland.com | Getting there By car, from I-4 E take exit 94 for W State Road 434, turn right onto Wekiva Springs Road and right onto Miami Springs Drive | Hours Sun–Thu 8am–7pm, Fri & Sat 8am–11pm | Tip For hiking, Wekiwa Springs State Park is nearby, with trails varying from under a mile to 13.5 miles (1800 Wekiwa Circle, Apopka, www.floridastateparks.org/parks-and-trails/wekiwa-springs-state-park).

109 Wells' Built Museum

Parramore's heritage center

For a place that once accommodated Count Basie, Ray Charles, Jackie Robinson, and Ella Fitzgerald, 511 W South Street is an unprepossessing building. But the Wells' Built Museum of African American History & Culture is much more than its humble confines suggest.

Built as a hotel in 1926 by Parramore's resident doctor William Monroe Wells (1889–1967), it tells the story of Orlando's Black community, its role in helping to establish the city, and how residents thrived despite segregation. Wells was a Black physician credited with delivering more than 5,000 babies in the district, and he was the only physician treating Black patients. He had already created the South Street Casino dance hall that attracted the biggest names of its time on the so-called Chitlin' Circuit of African American entertainers. But he realized they also needed a safe place to lodge under the Jim Crow laws of the time. So, he built one for them.

The hotel closed in 1957, a year after Wells' death, and it was destined for demolition until local history advocates Alzo Reddick and Geraldine Thompson mounted a campaign to transform it into a museum. Thompson, now a state senator, had collected a wealth of exhibits from her 24 years as assistant to the president of Valencia College, and the museum opened in 2009 with most of her material.

Now on the National Register of Historic Places, it is packed with 20th-century history, from its Hank Aaron memorabilia to a 1949 copy of the fabled *Green Book*. Look for a mock-up of a 1930s hotel room and a section devoted to Martin Luther King, Jr., who drew a crowd of more than 2,000 to Tinker Field on his only visit to Orlando in 1964. There are also key references to the Groveland Four, victims of appalling racial injustice in 1949; civil rights activist and college founder Mary McLeod Bethune; aviator Bessie Coleman; and to Wells himself.

The Fabric
of our
Communities

HISTORY IS CREATED
THROUGH MOMENTS IN TIME. THE
RELATIONSHIP BETWEEN PEOPLE AND
PLACES IS ESSENTIAL TO THE FABRIC
OF OUR COMMUNITY AND SHOULD
BE PRESERVED. A COMMUNITY'S
RIGHTS, IDENTITY, HISTORY AND
FUTURE ARE ALL INTERTWINED TO
CREATE ITS STORY AND PROTECT ITS
CULTURAL HERITAGE. RECOGNITION
AND PROTECTION OF SIGNIFICANT
BUILDINGS AND LANDSCAPES ALLOWS
US TO EXPLORE THE RICH HISTORY THAT
EXISTS IN ORLANDO'S BLACK AMERICAN
COMMUNITIES. WE INVITE YOU TO OPEN
YOUR EYES AND DISCOVER THESE
GREAT PLACES.

Address 511 W South Street, Orlando, FL 32805, +1 (407) 245-7535, www.wellsbuilt.org |
Getting there Bus 36, 62 to South Street & Chapman Court | Hours Mon–Fri 9am–5pm |
Tip Next door to the museum is the Dr. William Monroe Wells House. The house was
moved from its original 1920s spot to accommodate the Amway Center, home of the
Orlando Magic (519 W South Street, www.orlando.gov).

110 Wild Florida

Giraffes with attitude on a drive-thru Safari

Among Orlando's theme parks and other man-made attractions is a healthy sprinkling of nature and eco-friendly opportunities. Wild Florida really puts the "wild" in wildlife on the scenic shore of Cypress Lake south of Kissimmee, where two residents along the drive-thru safari really know how to engage with guests.

Starting with their signature airboat ride, Wild Florida blossomed into a well-rounded animal park and alligator habitat. It offers a home to various rescued and relocated animals, such as nuisance gators transferred here by the Florida Fish and Wildlife Conservation Commission, parrots surrendered by their owners, and other animals that cannot be returned to the wild. The 2019 addition of an 85-acre drive-through safari experience added more than 150 native and exotic animals. The venue eventually spread across 170 acres of savanna, earning it Central Florida's top spot for the largest family-owned adventure park. Species that make their home on the savanna have been chosen for their ability to thrive in Florida's climate and for their compatibility with other free-roaming animals.

But it's the giraffes Walter and Leroy who take their jobs as animal ambassadors seriously. Ten-year-old Walter is the park's biggest giraffe at 17 feet tall, and he is the star when it comes to grabbing guests' attention at the raised feeding station platform. He has a habit of licking their hands and ears, or using his 16-inch, prehensile tongue to latch on to guests' arms. Leroy, just three years old, patrols the safari grounds, keeping an eye on cars as they drive by, especially when there are children inside. If he wants a bit more attention, he'll lick the car's windshield. Leroy can often be seen touching noses as a sign of friendship with his buddy Mike the camel.

Other animals along the four-mile loop include wildebeest, Watusi cattle, water buffalo, ostriches, and zebras.

Address 3301 Lake Cypress Road, Kenansville, FL 34739, +1 (866) 532-7167, www.wildfloridairboats.com, info@wildfl.com | Getting there By car, take the Florida Turnpike south to exit 240 to Kissimmee Park Road. Turn right onto Old Canoe Creek Road, right onto Canoe Creek Road and right onto Lake Cypress Road. | Hours Mon–Sat 9am–6pm | Tip Kenansville's claim to fame is the Heartbreak Hotel, named for its once-shabby condition and not Elvis Presley's hit song (1350 S Canoe Creek Road, Kenansville).

111_ Yellow Dog Eats

The best doggone sandwich you'll ever taste

Local restaurants don't come more iconic than this delightfully quirky delicatessen in the rural suburb of Gotha. Built in 1910 as the Brockman House, it was converted into a café/antique shop with just 12 seats in 1999, but owner Fish Morgan's range of original sandwiches and salads proved so popular that he began to focus full-time on his menu. He quickly turned the restaurant into a local favorite.

The house itself was originally owned by Elise "Lizzie" Brockman, who purchased two lots of land that previously held a boarding house. She then had her own residence built, got married, and lived in Brockman House for the next seven years. From 1917 through 1925, the home changed owners several times and then spent the next 74 years cycling through various shops, including Gotha General Store. In 1999, Fish Morgan purchased the property, and it's been Yellow Dog Eats ever since.

Now with 89 seats, Yellow Dog has survived four fires, several hurricanes, a recession, and a pandemic, and it continues to flourish, thanks to Chef Morgan's freakish culinary combinations, such as the Berries 'n' Cream sandwich, a delicious mash-up of turkey, cream cheese, strawberry jam, cherry peppers, smoked bacon, and watercress on a toasted English muffin. He likely didn't learn *that* during his time at the Culinary Institute of America.

What about the restaurant's unusual name? Well, that's down to another mash-up, this time of Morgan's golden retriever and a family painting from his childhood.

Sit downstairs and peruse about 100 photographs of dogs, or dine upstairs, where the walls, tables, and chairs are covered in diners' signatures and scribbles, and the original Gotha General Store sign has pride of place. Or head outside for the intimate setting of The Garden for the best seats in the house. It's date night perfection, and you can bring your dog, too!

Address 1236 Hempel Avenue, Gotha, FL 34786, +1 (407) 296-0609,
www.yellowdogeats.com | Getting there By car, take the East-West Expressway (SR-408)
west to exit 2 and turn left onto Good Homes Road, right onto Old Winter Garden Road,
and left on Hempel Avenue | Hours Daily 11am–9pm | Tip Visit the random collection
of "statue alley," where Roman gladiators, zebras, charging horses, Christ on the cross, and
more can be viewed roadside (9957 8th Street, Gotha).

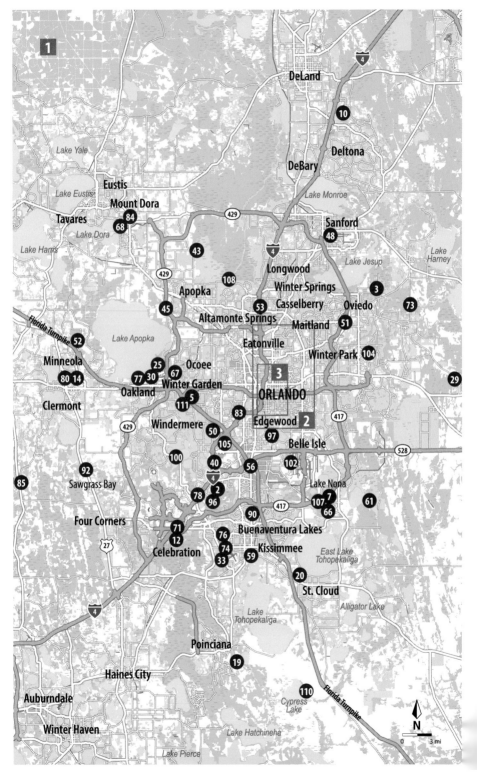

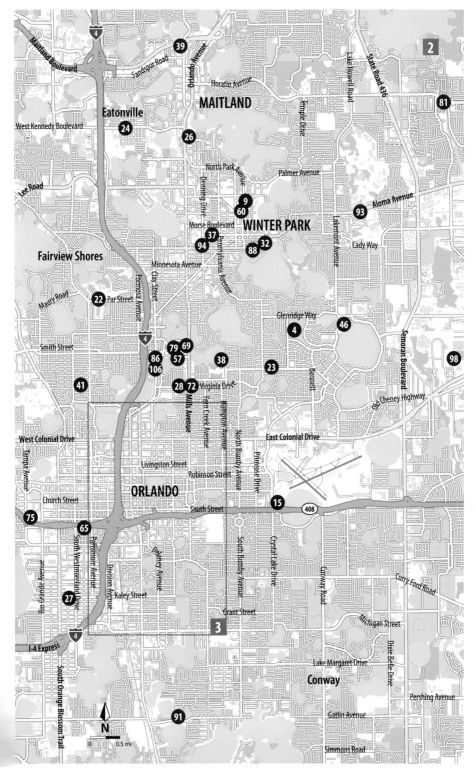

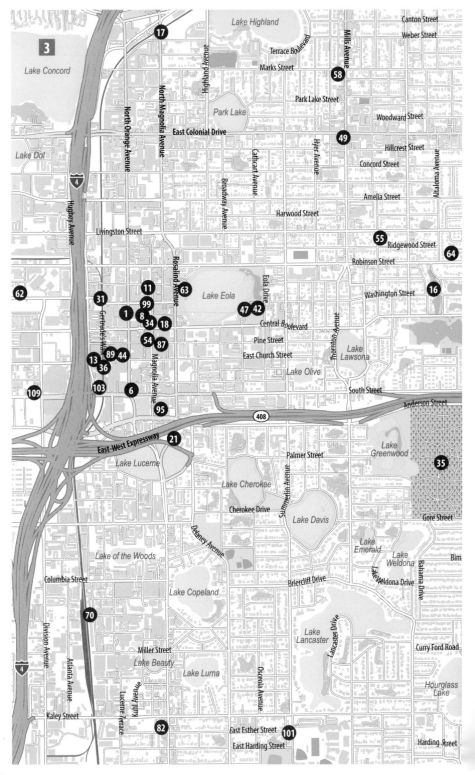

Jo-Anne Elikann, Susan Lusk
**111 Places in New York
That You Must Not Miss**
ISBN 978-3-7408-1888-3

Evan Levy, Rachel Mazor,
Joost Heijmenberg
**111 Places for Kids in New York
That You Must Not Miss**
ISBN 978-3-7408-1993-4

Wendy Lubovich, Ed Lefkowicz
**111 Museums in New York
That You Must Not Miss**
ISBN 978-3-7408-0379-7

Wendy Lubovich, Jean Hodgens
**111 Places in the Hamptons
That You Must Not Miss**
ISBN 978-3-7408-1891-3

Kim Windyka, Heather Kapplow,
Alyssa Wood
**111 Places in Boston
That You Must Not Miss**
ISBN 978-3-7408-1558-5

Brandon Schultz, Lucy Baber
**111 Places in Philadelphia
That You Must Not Miss**
ISBN 978-3-7408-1376-5

Andrea Seiger, John Dean
**111 Places in Washington
That You Must Not Miss**
ISBN 978-3-7408-1890-6

Kaitlin Calogera, Rebecca Grawl,
Cynthia Schiavetto Staliunas
**111 Places in Women's History
in Washington That You Must
Not Miss**
ISBN 978-3-7408-1590-5

Lauri Williamson, David Wardrick
**111 Places in Black Culture in
Washington, DC That You Must
Not Miss**
ISBN 978-3-7408-2003-9

Allison Robicelli, John Dean
111 Places in Baltimore
That You Must Not Miss
ISBN 978-3-7408-1696-4

Brian Hayden, Jesse Pitzler
111 Places in Buffalo
That You Must Not Miss
ISBN 978-3-7408-1440-3

Amy Bizzarri, Susie Inverso
111 Places in Chicago
That You Must Not Miss
ISBN 978-3-7408-1030-6

Michelle Madden, Janet McMillan
111 Places in Milwaukee
That You Must Not Miss
ISBN 978-3-7408-1643-8

Elizabeth Foy Larsen
111 Places in the Twin Cities
That You Must Not Miss
ISBN 978-3-7408-1347-5

Sandra Gurvis, Mitch Geiser
111 Places in Columbus
That You Must Not Miss
ISBN 978-3-7408-0600-2

Philip D. Armour, Susie Inverso
111 Places in Denver
That You Must Not Miss
ISBN 978-3-7408-1220-1

Travis Swann Taylor
111 Places in Atlanta
That You Must Not Miss
ISBN 978-3-7408-1887-6

Cristyle Egitto, Jakob Takos
111 Places in Palm Beach
That You Must Not Miss
ISBN 978-3-7408-1695-7

Dana DuTerroil, Joni Fincham,
Daniel Jackson
111 Places in Houston
That You Must Not Miss
ISBN 978-3-7408-2265-1

Dana DuTerroil, Joni Fincham,
Sara S. Murphy
111 Places for Kids in Houston
That You Must Not Miss
ISBN 978-3-7408-2267-5

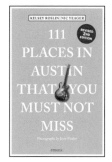

Kelsey Roslin, Nic Yeager,
Jesse Pitzler
111 Places in Austin
That You Must Not Miss
ISBN 978-3-7408-1642-1

Laurel Moglen, Julia Posey,
Lyudmila Zotova
111 Places in Los Angeles
That You Must Not Miss
ISBN 978-3-7408-1889-0

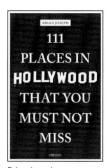

Brian Joseph
111 Places in Hollywood
That You Must Not Miss
ISBN 978-3-7408-1819-7

Floriana Petersen, Steve Werney
111 Places in San Francisco
That You Must Not Miss
ISBN 978-3-7408-2058-9

Floriana Petersen, Steve Werney
111 Places in Napa and Sonoma
That You Must Not Miss
ISBN 978-3-7408-1553-0

Floriana Petersen, Steve Werney
111 Places in Silicon Valley
That You Must Not Miss
ISBN 978-3-7408-1346-8

Harriet Baskas, Cortney Kelley
111 Places in Seattle
That You Must Not Miss
ISBN 978-3-7408-1992-7

Acknowledgements

We would like to thank Rose Garlick at Discover Downtown for her valuable insights and unending enthusiasm; historian Richard Forbes for his deep dives into Orlando's fascinating history; Amy Rodenbrock at Visit Orlando for the lunchtime meetings that always add to our repertoire of interesting places to visit; our dear friend Kevin Chippendale for tipping us off to some of the city's real gems; our photographer Kayla L. Smith for her beautiful work that brings each story to life; and our editor, Karen Seiger, for making it all happen.

Simon Veness has been in the journalism business since 1981, and was the original founder of the best-selling *Brit Guide* travel book series with UK publishers Foulsham in the mid-1990s. He developed the *Brit Guide to Orlando*, which delves into Central Florida's lesser-known attractions as well as the major theme parks, and *A Brit's Guide to Cruising.* He has a long history of contributing travel-related features to newspapers and magazines, including *The Telegraph*, *The Guardian*, *iNews*, and *The Independent.* He has featured on BBC TV's *Holiday* program and various regional radio stations, and continues to provide online blogs and content for a variety of outlets, including AttractionTickets.com, Real Florida Adventures, and Debbie's Villas, often highlighting offbeat and off-the-beaten-track locations.

Susan Veness is an international travel writer, solo author of three editions of *The Hidden Magic of Walt Disney World*, plus *Hidden Magic of Walt Disney World Trivia*, *The Hidden Magic of Walt Disney World Planner*, and *Walt Disney World Hacks.* Her eye for detail led her to become a contributor to a major unofficial Disney website and discussion forum, which she then parlayed into a job with the *Brit Guide* travel series as principal research assistant on their Orlando title in 2001, and later as editor for AttractionsMagazine.com. She has also contributed to a wide range of media outlets, from newspapers and magazines to online content.

Kayla L. Smith documented life as a teenager by taking Polaroid pictures. After purchasing her first DSLR, she discovered her love of photography and videography for capturing moments in people's lives in a way that would last forever. Today, her work has been featured in *The New York Times*, *People* Magazine, *Orlando Weekly*, and *Click* Magazine, and she has monthly articles in *Wild + Free* Magazine. She travels the country to photograph events, weddings, and family moments. Kayla lives in Orlando, and she draws her inspiration from God, who continues to expand her creativity, and also from the beautiful lives of those she loves. www.KaylaLSmith.com